T0372925

WHY WE ♥ THE MATRIX

WHY WE ♥

THE
MATRIX

KIM TAYLOR-FOSTER

RUNNING PRESS
PHILADELPHIA

Running Press
Hachette Book Group
1290 Avenue of the Americas, New York, NY 10104
www.runningpress.com
@Running_Press

Printed in China

First Edition: April 2021

Published by Running Press, an imprint of Perseus Books, LLC, a subsidiary of Hachette Book Group, Inc. The Running Press name and logo is a trademark of the Hachette Book Group.

The Hachette Speakers Bureau provides a wide range of authors for speaking events. To find out more, go to www.hachettespeakersbureau.com or call (866) 376-6591.

The publisher is not responsible for websites (or their content) that are not owned by the publisher.

Print book cover and interior design by Rachel Peckman

Library of Congress Control Number: 2020946886

ISBNs: 978-0-7624-7212-3 (hardcover), 978-0-7624-9855-0 (ebook)

RRD-S

10 9 8 7 6 5 4 3 2 1

For Adam, The Matrix's number-one fan

CONTENTS

WHY WE ♥ THE MATRIX

INTRODUCTION

The year 1999 was a landmark. The only time any adult alive today will have had the opportunity to celebrate the eve of one millennium dissolving into the dawn of the next. The new millennium wouldn't actually arrive for another twelve months officially, according to calendar authorities, but the world still partied hard as the year 2000 approached. Let that marinate for a moment. The last time the globe psyched up for the start of a new millennium, the world was in the middle of the Viking Age, and America hadn't been "discovered" yet.

A pivotal period in the digital revolution, in 1999, the World Wide Web really started to spread its roots. Making calls over the internet was beginning to catch on, music streaming service Napster launched, Bill Gates became the world's richest man amid rising demand from corporations for bandwidth, and high-speed connections took off. Plus, it was slap bang in the middle of the dotcom bubble. It was also the year that gave us *The Matrix*.

A film about a man named Thomas Anderson working a programming job for a generic software corporation who, by night, becomes computer hacker Neo, *The Matrix*, at first, appears deceptively simple. It isn't. A feeling that "there is something wrong with the world," leads Neo to discover the existence of an entity known as "the Matrix." However, it isn't until he's tracked down by the so-called terrorist Morpheus, a man Neo is intrigued by, and shiny vinyl-clad sidekick, Trinity, that he fully understands the nature of the Matrix. And the idea that his whole life has been a lie.

Digging into Hearts and Minds

Coming off the back of a bunch of what Hollywood director and *Matrix* actor Leigh Whannell calls "netsploitation" films, *The Matrix* and its vernacular, story, themes, and, of course, visuals still hold up today. There's a reason we still talk about the film decades after the film's creators, the Wachowskis, first uploaded it into our brains, and that's because it's really, really good. And by *good,* we mean layered, complex, detailed, rich, enigmatic. Oh, and did we forget really, really good looking?

Ask any fan and they'll tell you the groundbreaking visual effects and its captivating story are what drew them to the movie. But it's the film's knotty philosophy and labyrinthine mythology that drove it, and continue to drive it, deep into our hearts (and minds)—a bit like the digger machines of *The Matrix Reloaded* boring into Zion. *The Matrix* is a gift to cinephiles, one that keeps on giving by raising questions that our minds continue to contemplate as the years pass. It's no surprise that, sixteen years after the sequels helped fully embed the world of *The Matrix* into moviegoers' consciousness, a fourth was announced.

When *The Matrix* first hit screens, audiences were amazed. As the world approached the new millennium—the very millennium referenced in seminal works of screen science fiction, including *Blade Runner, 2001, Metropolis*, and more—minds were turned to the future and humankind's increasing dependence on technology in the digital age. *The Matrix* followed in the footsteps of numerous sci-fi tales in which machines go bad—*The Terminator, Westworld, Demon Seed, Tron*, and 1984 romantic sci-fi dramedy *Electric Dreams*, to name just a few. And as the new millennium loomed, it brought with it fears of the millennium bug, thought set to crash global computer networks, as well as apprehension around advanced tech and our growing reliance on it. That's on top of burgeoning trepidation that the likelihood of artificial intelligence achieving sentience and turning on us was quite possibly *not* just the stuff of fiction. We were primed for this resonant tale. And resonate it did.

Leigh Whannell played Axel in *The Matrix* franchise and has gone on to become a successful writer-director in Hollywood of both science fiction and horror movies. Whannell created both the *Saw* franchise and *Upgrade*, the latter of which, a futuristic neo-noir revenge thriller about a man trapped in a "different reality," explores the same themes of control and technophobia as *The Matrix*. The director has shared his thoughts on why we love *The Matrix*, noting that such is his own admiration for the film, he needs at least an hour to discuss it, impossible as it is for him to talk in sound bites about the Wachowskis' masterpiece.

"With movies that become these pop culture totems, there's usually a combination of things. It's like a perfect smoothie, to make a terrible food analogy. If you have a little bit too much of this or that it doesn't taste as good. It has to be the perfect combination of ingredients. *The Matrix*, I think, is that. It has that striking image of Keanu Reeves with the sunglasses and the black trench coat, and then there's this unique way of shooting fight scenes—the bullet time [effect]. It's presenting, essentially, an old story—the hero that gets plucked

out of nowhere to save the world—but dressed up
in new clothing.

"*The Matrix*, I felt, was *Star Wars* for the early
millennial generation and it was also the first film,
on a large scale anyway, to really incorporate this
brave new world of the internet into a movie. I
remember when the internet first became a thing in
the mid-nineties, there was this rash of 'netsploitation'
films. I remember the Sandra Bullock one, *The Net*.
And *Hackers,* with Angelina Jolie rollerblading
around. It would always be this hilarious early
netspeak that they would get wrong. I've got a clip
on my Twitter account of Julia Stiles [in the 1990s
TV series, *Ghostwriter*] saying, 'Can you jam with
the console cowboys in cyberspace?' As if that's how
hackers talk.

"*The Matrix* was the first film to [convincingly]
tackle this new world that is now so ubiquitous in
our lives. Twenty years later, there's not a person out
there on the street from an 80-year-old man to a
six-year-old girl who doesn't know what the internet
is, and spends half their life staring at this black mirror.
I felt *The Matrix* plugged into the idea of another
reality; it was an early adopter of this idea that the
internet of the virtual world would become another
reality that we could live in. And now it kind of is."

Loved Then and Now

So how did it land with audiences? The film had its detractors, sure—like many works of art that aren't immediately understood or appreciated in their own time—but critics and moviegoers alike praised plenty of the elements the film is still lauded for today. The *New York Times* noted that "the martial arts dynamics are phenomenal" and complimented the Wachowskis for the way they "stylishly envision the ultimate in cyberescapism, creating a movie that captures the duality of life à la laptop."

The *Los Angeles Times* said: "A wildly cinematic futuristic thriller that is determined to overpower the imagination, *The Matrix* combines traditional science fiction premises with spanking new visual technology in a way that almost defies description." Roger Ebert called it a "visually dazzling cyberadventure, full of kinetic excitement." Then, just a year after its release, Ian Nathan would write in *Empire*: "In the clearest sense of the term *The Matrix* is a classic, not only a great movie, but a film that simultaneously redefined its own medium. Forever."

In the days before internet forums and social media were widespread, most moviegoers simply let their money do the talking—the film's box office receipts are proof that old-fashioned word of mouth (with a little help from reviews and marketing) had done its job, driving film fans in their droves to theaters. Not that there was a dearth of online chatter.

Wherever movie fans gathered in the digital space, they shared their thoughts. One IMDb user, mambubukid, posted shortly after its release that *The Matrix* is "the definitive hybrid of technical wizardry and contextual excellence that should be the benchmark for all sci-fi films to come." Others called it "one of the best films ever" and "stunning and wild." Another said, "The more you watch it, the better it gets."

Fans still love it hard for the reasons it captured their imaginations in the first place. Search Twitter, sneak a peek on Fandom, or visit Reddit, and you'll find people still referencing the film and espousing its virtues today. Whether repeating its messages to "wake up" or signposting the present-day relevance of Smith's "Virus" speech, in which he likens humans to a "disease," it's clear that so many of us love *The Matrix*. From its cast and characters to its thought-provoking themes and blend of practical action with cutting-edge visual effects, here are the reasons why.

When Morpheus speaks, Neo listens.
Heck, when Morpheus speaks, we all listen.
If you were to live by the words of
Morpheus alone, you'd be doing all right.
Probably even winning at life. Here's the first
of many sage sayings from the Resistance's
inspirational leader you'll find throughout this
book that you can use as a guide to help
you navigate your existence.
Don't thank us, thank Morpheus.

THE WISDOM OF MORPHEUS

"There's a difference between knowing the path and walking the path."

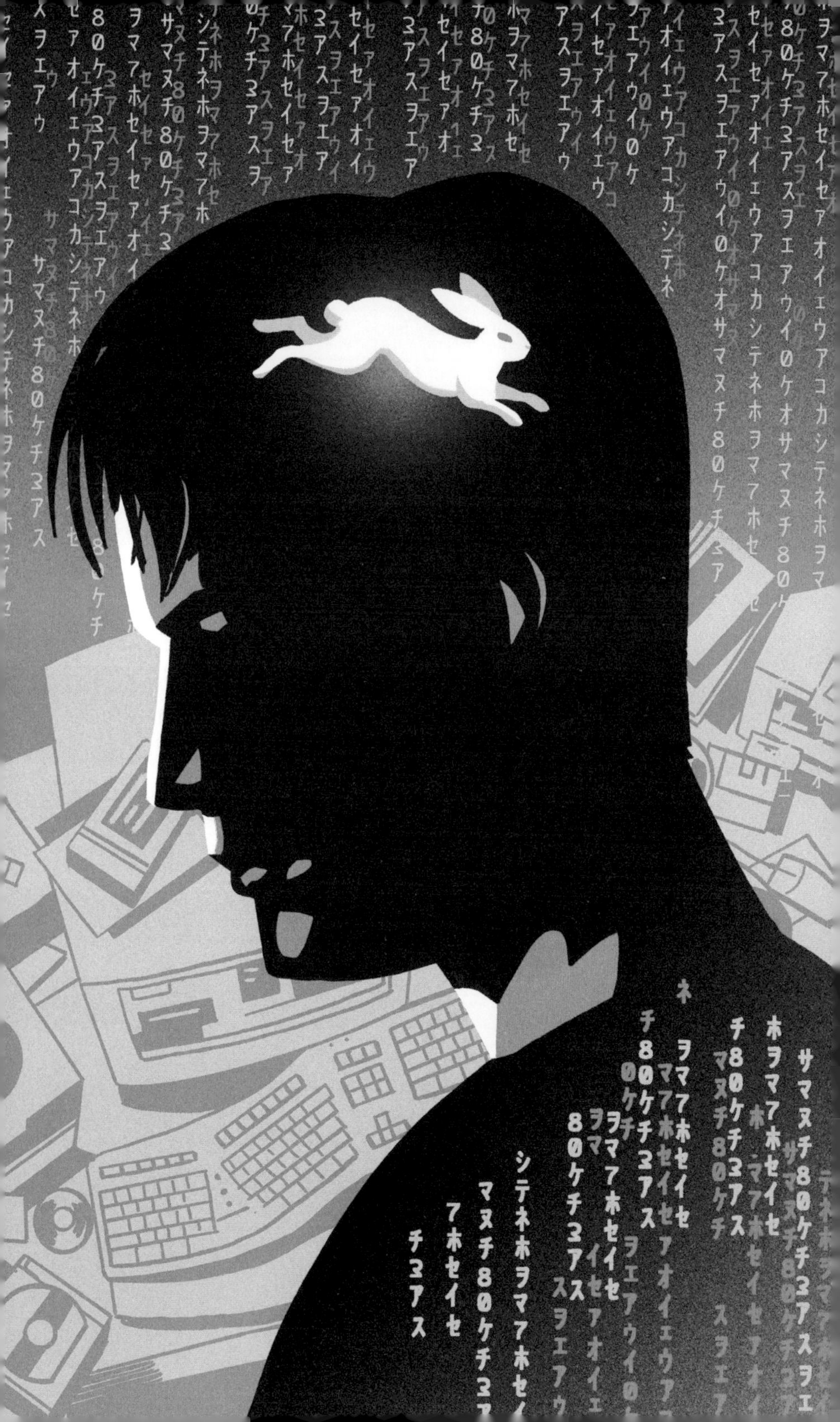

CHAPTER 1

Booting Up *The Matrix*

I t's funny how things pan out. If Eric Stoltz had played
Marty McFly as per the original plan instead of Michael J.
Fox, we'd have an entirely different *Back to the Future*. If
Harrison Ford hadn't been building a door in the American
Zoetrope offices when George Lucas was casting *Star Wars*,
Han Solo might not have become the cinema icon he turned
into (Kurt Russell, Christopher Walken, and Al Pacino were
all considered; at the very least, you're looking at a very
different take on the roguish space pirate). And never mind
the fact that a couple of studios passed on the film before
20th Century Fox finally said yes, throwing the whole
existence of *Star Wars* into doubt in the first place. What, no
Star Wars? Unimaginable.

Then there's *The Wizard of Oz*. If the screenplay hadn't
undergone several rewrites and a change of director no fewer
than three times, the film wouldn't have gone on to become
an enduring classic of cinema. And what about *Blade Runner*?
Had Ridley Scott's masterpiece not had a rewrite, an increase
in budget, and a producer swoop in and save the picture when
its backers, erm, backed out, it wouldn't have gotten made.

As for *The Matrix*, it had its own almost-didn't-happen tale. If the Wachowskis hadn't had their precious creative digits singed prior to working on their own masterpiece, when their script for the Richard Donner–directed *Assassins* was completely retooled, and if they hadn't been encouraged to make their violent neo-noir showcase *Bound* in the interim, in turn finding themselves buoyed by its modest success, things could have gone very differently. With a competent genre picture to their name, and armed with firsthand knowledge of how brutal Hollywood could be, they remained steadfast when selling and then directing their screenplay for *The Matrix*. Without circumstances falling into place, we would likely have ended up with another forgettable '90s netsploitation dud for Leigh Whannell to roll his eyes at.

Come to think of it, would the film even have been *conceived* if *any* of the above hadn't transpired? If *Star Wars*, *The Wizard of Oz*, *Blade Runner*, and *Back to the Future* hadn't become the films we know and love today? All had a colossal impact on *The Matrix*, a film created from and strengthened immeasurably by its influences and intricate network of homages and references.

The influence of *Star Wars* on *The Matrix* can be seen in its shared scope, conception as a trilogy, and pioneering use of visual effects; *Blade Runner* in its similarly bleak neo-noir futurescape; and *The Wizard of Oz* in Neo's Dorothy-esque immersion in (and emergence from) a dream world. *The Matrix*'s Oracle can also be seen as a version of the Wizard, while the green code and tint of the Matrix itself recalls Oz's Emerald City (both worlds are united in their standing as elaborate hoaxes). *The Wizard of Oz* is even referenced directly by Cypher in *The Matrix* when he says, "Buckle your seat belt, Dorothy, 'cause Kansas is going bye-bye."

But while the influence of these films can be seen in their similarities, *Back to the Future*'s impact is measured in its differences. Robert Zemeckis's era-defining 1980s presentation of the future—bright colors, hoverboards, and flying cars, not too far-removed from Keanu Reeves's own time-traveling sci-fi comedies *Bill and Ted's Excellent Adventure* (1989) and its sequel, *Bogus Journey* (1991)—are in stark contrast to the darker turn *The Matrix* took. *The Matrix* is in some ways a reaction to a presentation of the future that had become prevalent. Interestingly, though, the Wachowskis would embrace color and playfulness in later works, *Speed Racer* and *Jupiter Ascending*.

A Perfect Storm

For *The Matrix* to exist in the form it took, it needed a perfect storm, composed of each and every one of these fateful outcomes, and more. But despite its many, varied influences and all the cogs slotting into place, it's fair to say that *The Matrix* wouldn't have come to fruition if it weren't for the Wachowskis' own personal questioning of their identities. Since first Lana and then Lilly Wachowski came out to the world as trans people, commentators have reexamined their seminal work through a different lens. In 2020, Lilly Wachowski finally revealed that she and Lana had always intended for the film to be a trans allegory.

If artists put themselves into their work, then *The Matrix* is the uncluttering of a pair of overloaded, inquisitive minds. Wachowski DNA is practically spliced into the film. At one point during production, Belinda McClory's character, Switch, was intended to be a woman in the Matrix and a man in real life, and the themes of identity, duality, the power of the mind, and truth are strong examples that suggest the Wachowskis were consciously or unconsciously exploring themselves. Lilly Wachowski would tell Netflix in 2020: "The Matrix stuff was all about the desire for transformation but it was all coming from a closeted point of view . . . [I don't know] how present my transness was in the background of my brain as we were writing."

But it isn't just their questioning of their identities that weighed heavily on their minds—there's so much philosophy, religion, futurism, and other musings stuffed into *The Matrix*, it's as if the siblings wanted to tap into everything they'd ever pondered. They've even admitted as much: "Every idea we've ever had in our entire lives is in this film," said Lana back in 1999. Essentially, *The Matrix* is the Wachowskis' self-contained oeuvre. It's a mash-up of deeply personal struggles, big philosophical ideas, and homages and references to a cornucopia of existing films and books—all the things that meant anything to them—and consequently, the film was always going to find its place in our hearts and minds.

TECHNOPHOBIA

The rise of artificial intelligence and the fear of technology were increasingly infiltrating people's thoughts in 1999. Among a handful of less-than-credible netsploitation films coming through at the end of the nineties (*Hackers*; *The Net*; *Johnny Mnemonic*, starring Keanu Reeves; even the Tom Hanks–Meg Ryan romantic drama *You've Got Mail*), *The Matrix* feels like the only one to take on and tackle the theme properly.

Tapping into our ever-increasing fear of technology, and the specific worry around the Y2K "millennium bug" that was projected to strike at the turn of the year 2000, the film predicted a world where vast swaths of the population would be "plugged in" to virtual worlds for huge portions of time and explored a culture that was built off our creations of different personas for our online lives. Even Morpheus, Neo, Trinity, et al. get to choose their "avatars" inside the Matrix via their "residual self-image."

It's a phenomenon that reverberates all the louder now that we know the Wachowskis themselves were battling with their own identities. Allowing some people an outlet for exploring their real selves, technology has also proven, in the years since *The Matrix*'s release, to have a much darker side. From the rise of online influencers and the portrayal of "perfection" that has been linked to an increase in anxiety and depression and, worse, suicide, to the murky recesses of the Dark Web and cybercrime, it's clear the internet can be a bad place.

The march of progress is presented in *The Matrix* as the route to our own demise—more pertinent than ever in the increasing panic over climate change and fear of influential fingers hovering resolutely over red buttons. "Human beings are a disease, a cancer of this planet," says Smith. It's a powerfully delivered message and one that puts our actions in sharp relief. He's not wrong—if we wipe out humans, we'd solve many of the world's ills. Only problem is, we wouldn't be here to enjoy it.

Hard Work, Belief, and Synchronicity

Partly because of the expansive ambition and density of the project, the screenplay for *The Matrix* was a problem. Few who got a sniff of it understood this complex, cerebral sci-fi actioner, but circumstances and timing aligned to get the Wachowskis' mystifying vision to the screen. Just like Morpheus, whose unwavering faith in fate—or, at least, the fate we make for ourselves—contributes to making sure things come to pass, the Wachowskis' determination to make *The Matrix* their way paid off.

Lorenzo di Bonaventura at Warner Bros. had already bought the rights to the screenplay for *The Matrix*, and he believed in the Wachowskis' script, but he knew that others needed persuading. It was on his advice that the duo made *Bound* first, believing that what they did with the film would go some way toward selling *The Matrix* by proving them competent, if not masterful, filmmakers.

Bound was, like *The Matrix*, a neo-noir, set in a kind of modern-day alternate universe. It took a fresh approach to the mob movie, pushing the femme fatale front and center into the protagonist role and subverting conventions. Both Gina

Gershon and Jennifer Tilly, who starred in the film (alongside *The Matrix*'s Cypher, Joe Pantoliano), have more than a touch of Trinity about them in their appearances—short raven hair and inky leather abound. As with *The Matrix*, the Wachowskis played with innovative cinematography; there's even use of slow motion, a kind of rudimentary antecedent to the *Matrix*'s bullet-time technique they would go on to develop. Color, too, marked itself out as important in their work for the first time: a limited palette of mainly black, white, and red adds a hyperreality to proceedings and signifies a multitude of things, including varyingly control, freedom, and danger. In *Bound*, it was possible to see the kind of filmmakers they were and the type of film they could make out of their *Matrix* screenplay.

"When you read the [*Matrix*] script, you knew it was a new and different kind of movie," di Bonaventura told the *New York Times* at the time of *The Matrix*'s release. "It had great action and great characters, and you got a sense of how important these filmmakers would become."

He added, "A few of us didn't find it incomprehensible and felt the [sisters] would be able to execute visually what some people had a hard time understanding when they read it."

However, despite the success of *Bound*, execs still weren't quite ready to take a punt on *The Matrix*. Having originally intended for *The Matrix* to be a comic book—Lana had a job working on comic books at the time—now seemed the right time to enlist the help of some valuable contacts to bring the visuals in their minds to life. Artist Geof Darrow created some designs for the film's forbidding tech, while former colleague Steve Skroce was tasked with putting together nearly six hundred storyboards to showcase the movie.

It took this—alongside the failure of the über-expensive *Batman and Robin*—to convince Warner Bros. that audiences had had their fill of by-numbers sequels and "same-old, same-old," and were thirsty for new, original content. Meaning that *The Matrix*, with its $60 million budget, was now good to go. The clincher was that they wouldn't, at least, lose money on it. Warner Bros. needn't have worried, of course. The Wachowskis, taking their prior experience of the industry and learnings from *Bound* into their virtual reality–themed project, would provide an antidote to *Batman and Robin* as they wrote even more lines into the film's source code for a formula audiences were guaranteed to fall for.

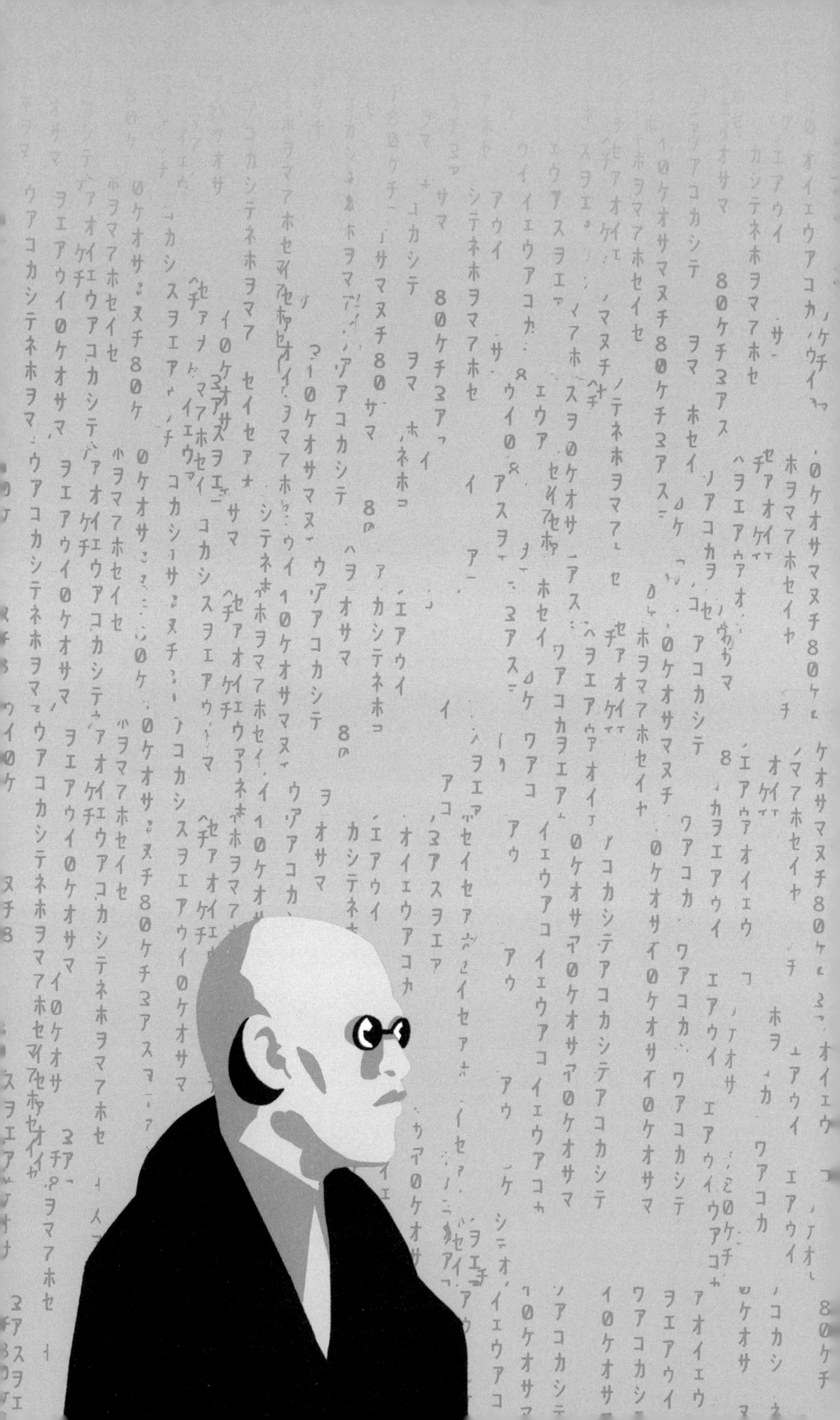

THE WISDOM OF MORPHEUS

"You take the Blue Pill, the story ends. You wake up in your bed and believe whatever you want to believe. You take the Red Pill, you stay in Wonderland, and I show you how deep the rabbit hole goes."

SYMBOLISM: RED AND MIRRORS

The Matrix is rich in symbolism, from the name of the company Neo / Thomas Anderson works for—Meta Cortechs / MetaCortex, which roughly means "transcending the limits of the mind"—to other metaphors we'll explore in this book. But you'll also find the color red and mirror motifs scattered throughout, respectively issuing a warning or signifier of change and reflecting a sense of a plurality of both existence and identity.

Instances of red are multiple in *The Matrix*. Some of the most interesting include the red matchbox prominent in the bowl of Neo's apartment at the beginning, just before he hears a knock on the door and his adventure down the rabbit hole begins; Morpheus's red leather chair as we're deciding whether we can trust him; the red man on a traffic light just after Cypher has expressed doubt about Neo and Morpheus; and, of course, the Red Pill and the woman in the red dress.

Examples of mirrors used symbolically include Neo reflected in both Morpheus's and Cypher's shades (both lenses); Neo's duality visualized in a cracked mirror, which becomes fluid as his hand merges with it; and Neo's image reflected in the

back of the spoon, which distorts and bends with
the spoon as Spoon Boy manipulates it.

The Significance of Its Influences and References

The Matrix was accused by some at the time of its release
of ripping off Alex Proyas's *Dark City*, which had come out
the year before, covered similar ground, and whose sets the
Wachowskis borrowed for filming. This move, alongside the
decision to shoot in Australia instead of the United States,
kept the Wachowskis to the $60 million budget rather than
the then record $180 million it would otherwise have cost.
It proved to be very shrewd not only financially but also in
terms of amplifying the film's themes. What better way to
explore the concept of a constructed virtual reality than by
using the blueprint set by another film exploring similar topics?

Both movies' plots revolve around the idea that humanity
has been enslaved, unknowingly, within an elaborately
constructed illusion, created by other beings, and both deal
with the themes of identity, love, and reality. In *The Matrix*,
however, humanity's fate is of our own making—we built the
machines—while in *Dark City*, the humans are enslaved and
exploited by aliens from another world. Shared sets comprised
various buildings and exteriors, including rooftops—those
that Trinity runs across at the beginning of *The Matrix* are the
same that Rufus Sewell's John Murdoch hurdles in *Dark City*.

In leaning into this mirroring, the Wachowskis firstly highlight a sameness and artificiality to the concept of virtual worlds. Secondly, they acknowledge philosopher Jean Baudrillard's writings, in which they were interested, about the "simulacrum"—defined as something that replaces reality with its representation. Thirdly, they begin to construct a feeling of familiarity, a kind of déjà vu that works with the film's multiple references to other works to help us read the film's symbolism and themes. This at the same time as working in their very own meta-glitch in *The Matrix*.

As we learned earlier, *Dark City* is far from the only film or influence *The Matrix* channels. Since we've already touched on films like *Star Wars*, *The Wizard of Oz*, *Blade Runner*, and *Back to the Future*, let's explore some of the other works of pop culture and beyond that are hardwired into *The Matrix*.

HOW THE WACHOWSKIS MAKE US REFLECT

The Wachowskis use a number of techniques and moments throughout the film to continually encourage us to reflect on our own lives. One method is self-reflexivity—drawing attention to the artifice of what we see on-screen. References to other works drop us straight back into our own lives by breaking our immersion in the fictional world as we register the acknowledgment. We align *The Matrix* with these other works, which amplifies the themes and helps us to both understand and apply them to our own lives.

A good example of multiple references stacked into just one scene is when Neo meets Spoon Boy and the other potentials. The sequence itself is a callback to the end of *Akira*, but there are also giant rabbits on the TV screen in the scene. The clip is from the film *Night of the Lepus*. At the same time, the footage acknowledges *Alice in Wonderland*, one of the film's major influences, which it references on more than one occasion.

Alice in Wonderland and *Night of the Lepus* both exist in the *Matrix* universe as they do in ours, which means we can infer that *The Matrix* operates within our universe. This helps us to more easily imagine *The Matrix* as a future version of our own world. Additionally, nods to rich, symbolic works of fiction like *Akira* and *Alice in Wonderland* serve to equate *The Matrix* with them. It's impossible to miss the parallels with *Alice*—just as Alice is taken out of her familiar, ill-fitting existence to awaken in a new world of discovery, so is Neo. And just as *Akira* is a postapocalyptic cyberpunk story exploring themes such as control, destruction, religion, and rebirth, so is *The Matrix*. The metaphors of the earlier works are subsequently transplanted to the Wachowskis' film to encourage the audience to interpret the film in similar ways, or inspire us to draw parallels between them. It's a powerful way of driving the Wachowskis' messages home.

The Wachowskis are not only screen literate, they're also well read, and they pack a bunch of nods to other works into their very own masterwork that help to enrich what we see, and what we take from what we see on-screen. While *The Matrix* has the cyberpunk aesthetic of highbrow sci-fi authors J. G. Ballard, Philip K. Dick, and William Gibson, it also references middlebrow movies like *Total Recall*, *The Terminator*, and *Terminator 2*, and even 1995's lower-yet-brow *Hackers*. The name and concept of "the Matrix" itself isn't even original—a similar program known by the same name appeared in an episode of *Doctor Who* in 1976. And this is to say nothing of the written works of philosophers René Descartes, Plato, Socrates, and Jean Baudrillard, whose book *Simulcra and Simulation* not only inspired the film in part but is also *in it* (it's the hollowed-out tome Neo keeps his contraband inside at his apartment). Other books including Kevin Kelly's *Out of Control: The New Biology of Machines, Social Systems, and the Economic World* and Dylan Evans's *Introducing Evolutionary Psychology* were set alongside Baudrillard as Keanu Reeves's reading homework before filming began.

You'll also find nods to anime classics *Akira* and *Ghost in the Shell*, as well as Bruce Lee films. There's even a self-aware allusion to *Bill and Ted* in there, as the Wachowskis stake a claim for the responsibility of taking Keanu Reeves and turning him into a bona fide icon of cinema. From dumb surfer dude to kung fu–kicking savior of the human race, a well-placed "Whoa" in the script reminds us unapologetically, and quite deliberately, where he came from.

There are too many influences and references to create a comprehensive list here. Suffice it to say that each and every homage and callback serves to add depth to the film and underline *The Matrix*'s messages and themes. "They're taking all of the old stuff and trying to present it in a modern context," said Laurence Fishburne of the Wachowskis' work on the film. With the Wachowskis exploring Baudrillard's ideas in *The Matrix*, it makes sense that they wanted to make *The Matrix* a "copy," or to use Baudrillard's term, "simulacrum," of the works that came before it.

Assimilating so many other works and ideas may be a deliberate act to turn *The Matrix* into a likeness of what's gone before, but nevertheless, the Wachowskis also managed to turn their hodgepodge into something that still feels fresh and relevant—a work of art that audiences, both then and now, respond to in new ways. It's a smart move. Some might say genius. It certainly meant the film was better able to tap into the era and people's fears and excitement around revolutionary technology and the future. The Wachowskis were able to reflect and amplify the thoughts and feelings of the populace, while also drawing audiences into conversations they wanted them to continue, like how far we have free will, how much we are controlled, how dangerous artificial intelligence might be, and what constitutes identity. While, at the same time, fairly accurately predicting an epoch, twenty years later, when the line between reality and virtual reality is increasingly blurred and our dependence on being "plugged in" is greater than ever.

These myriad references also go some way toward building in a sense of déjà vu: *The Matrix*'s very own glitch. Why do we love *The Matrix*? It's coded into the film's programming that we love it, with Wachowski blood, sweat, tears, and sheer determination stitched in, alongside all the references and works we already know and love.

CHAPTER 2
Neo-Natal: The Birth of an Icon

The moment when Neo awakens for the first time from his digital slumber gets burned onto your retinas, branded into your brain. Among *The Matrix*'s many innovative visuals, this is one that makes a visceral impression no matter how many times you've seen it. And not just because of the sight of a hairless Keanu Reeves, shorn of his trademark locks, his dark, face-framing brows, and—latterly—his black, wispy, signature beard. Though that *is* pretty shocking—Reeves said of the "defuzzing" that people had trouble looking him in the eye.

In 1999, when *The Matrix* was first released, Reeves was best known as shaggy-do'd slacker Ted "Theodore" Logan from the *Bill and Ted* movies and as tall, dark, handsome undercover surfer cop Johnny Utah, from Kathryn Bigelow's *Point Break*, just two of the defining moments in a career that has both confounded and delighted audiences.

The Matrix is the film in which Keanu Reeves finally hit his stride and audiences caught up with him. Previously criticized for a perceived lack of acting ability; for possessing looks over both talent and brains—despite a string of high-profile and eclectic roles in some acclaimed films (*My Own Private Idaho*, anyone?)—when the role of Neo landed, high kicking and primal screaming onto screens, things clicked. His signature delivery and style, which some read as "blank," made him the perfect fit for a bleak, noir-ish, futuristic, cyberpunk tale about technology taking over and that muddied the line between fantasy and reality.

Indeed, it's not a million miles away from another breakthrough sci-fi neo-noir from the preceding decade. Harrison Ford's laconic delivery cemented *Blade Runner*'s protagonist, Rick Deckard, as one of cinema's most memorable, and important, pop culture icons for many of the same reasons. As humankind's aptly low-key savior, Neo, Reeves fit the bill to a T—and it's still the role for which he's arguably most lauded. It's no surprise that his career plateaued for a period after his stint as Neo, as industry chiefs and audiences alike were unable to figure out where to take him and what to make of him post-*Matrix*. Of course, Reeves is now riding the crest of a wave, enjoying success with another pop-culture franchise icon, John Wick, which is heavily influenced by *The Matrix*.

KNOCK, KNOCK, NEO

At the beginning of *The Matrix*, when we first
see Keanu Reeves, he's receiving messages on his
computer from a mystery correspondent. The words
Knock, knock, Neo appear on the screen, then *Follow
the white rabbit*, right before he hears a knock at his
door. Keanu Reeves would later star in a film called
Knock, Knock, directed by Eli Roth, in which he
opens the door to two strangers and a whole
different rabbit hole, inviting a heap of trouble into
his world. If *The Matrix* is in part about self-
fulfilling prophecies—here's one in real life.

Big, Bald Baby

Keanu Reeves is so intrinsically linked with the role of Neo, it's hard to think of any other actor bringing quite the same dynamic. "When I first read that script, it made my blood happy," Reeves is quoted as saying, while franchise directors, the Wachowskis, said, "We knew it would take a maniacal commitment from someone, and Keanu was that maniac." If happy blood doesn't signal maniacal commitment, it's hard to imagine what does. Reeves was so maniacally committed, in fact, that he remained devoted to the role through major surgery on his back ahead of filming, which put him out of action for months.

So what of those other Neo contenders? Most famously, perhaps, Will Smith turned down the role in favor of big-budget mega-flop *Wild Wild West*, but he wasn't the only big name associated with the part. Brad Pitt, Leonardo DiCaprio, Val Kilmer, and Johnny Depp were also considered—as was Reeves's *Speed* costar Sandra Bullock, whose Thomasina Anderson would have put an entirely different spin on the character.

But let's go back to *that* scene. We've established that Keanu Reeves was right for the role. So how do you make Keanu Reeves even more of a "blank" slate onto which to project your theme-stuffed movie about technology becoming sentient and taking over? Make him a big, bald baby, breaking out of an amniotic sac and ripping out the umbilical cord that plugs him into his previous existence, yanking him from his "safe" bubble into "real" life. That's how.

Of course, "Neo" means "new"—hence the rebirth scene, in which he whooshes along a tube, plunges into then emerges from a pool of water, before being pulled through an opening and into a shaft of light. Neo is also an anagram of "one." Neo *is* the One; he's also the *new* "One," as we'll eventually discover in the sequels—the sixth iteration of the One, destined to succeed in overthrowing the machines where others failed.

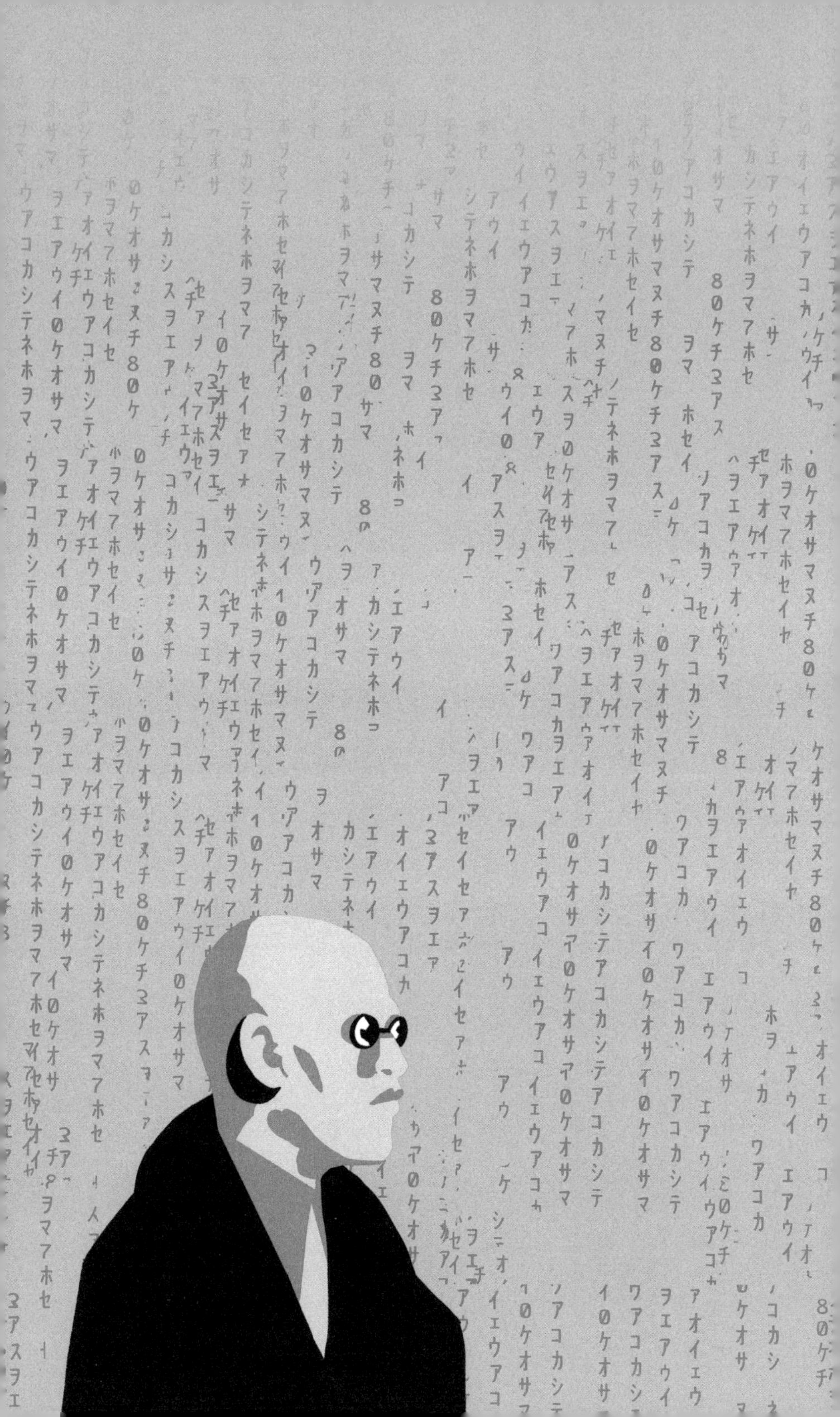

THE WISDOM OF MORPHEUS

"You have the look of a man
who accepts what he sees
because he is expecting to
wake up. Ironically, this is not
far from the truth."

Everyman Audience Surrogate

WHY WE LOVE THE MATRIX

But Neo isn't just a hero. He isn't just the prophesied One but also a dissatisfied everyman, representative of every *one* of *us* resentful of and disillusioned by, knowingly or unknowingly, the workings of the civilized world. Every one of us that has been, and is, a slave to the system, which is a social construction. In the early scenes of the film, we see Neo with a pallid, gray-white complexion; he's set against angular, beige offices and among colorless coworkers and walks sleepily through his existence. It's in Neo we see ourselves.

There's a reason that Neo asks forty-four questions in the eighty lines he speaks during the first third of the film's running time. We're being told to keep questioning, actively discouraged from becoming entrenched in blind acceptance, in order to seek out truth so that we can be truly free.

Crucially, too, Neo is humble, *normal*—just like most of us see ourselves. When he's told he's special—that he's the One—he doesn't believe it. Then, when the Oracle tells him he's not, it's incontrovertible proof to him that Morpheus is wrong to tell him differently. "Reluctant hero" is all of us, all over. In the beginning of the film, his ill-fitting suit is indicative of the idea that he doesn't fit into the (virtual) world that he's clearly at odds with, and we see him transform through the franchise into the hero he's fated to be, with the clothes to match, as he moves closer toward fulfilling his destiny. Ultimately, Neo is the hero everybody needs—back then in 1999, within the franchise universe, and right now more than ever.

SIX SPOONS

When Neo meets the potential widely known as Spoon Boy, the wise youngster is seen to have six spoons laid out on the carpet in front of him. Five of these are twisted into abstract shapes; the sixth, he picks up, bends, reshapes, and hands to Neo. We find out in the sequels that Neo is the sixth iteration of the One. It's worth mentioning that there is also a display case of spoons on the wall.

Neo, like Keanu Reeves, isn't *only* a blank slate, of course. He isn't *only* a simple two-dimensional, universalized protagonist for us all to project ourselves onto. If that's all he was, he wouldn't be the cinematic icon that he is today. Indeed, Neo has a sense of humor and an innate distrust of and disregard for authority. When he gives Agent Smith the finger during the interrogation scene, we both laugh and applaud him.

Neo also, critically, has a sense of what's cool. He's wowed by the idea that Morpheus (and he himself) can jump inhuman distances, and he's bowled over by the fact that he has learned kung fu through a computer simulation.

He's eminently likable because of down-to-earth personality traits we admire: he's funny, willing to have a go, questions authority, and thinks cool things are cool. But if you need more evidence that the film was ahead of its time, it's interesting to note the meta touches inherent in Neo, before being meta in mainstream movies became widespread.

Neo is equated with the wide-eyed science fiction fans sitting in front of the cinema screen, taking in the film's astonishing special effects, the likes of which they'd never seen before. By embodying the characteristics of fan culture before being a "geek" was considered cool, the character of Neo has been unequivocally instrumental in shifting the culture from the underground to the mainstream and shaping modern attitudes toward deeply engaged fandoms. Neo is not only the ultimate superhero in the world of the Matrix—with abilities that transcend all comers—he's also in possession of powers that extend beyond the movie screen.

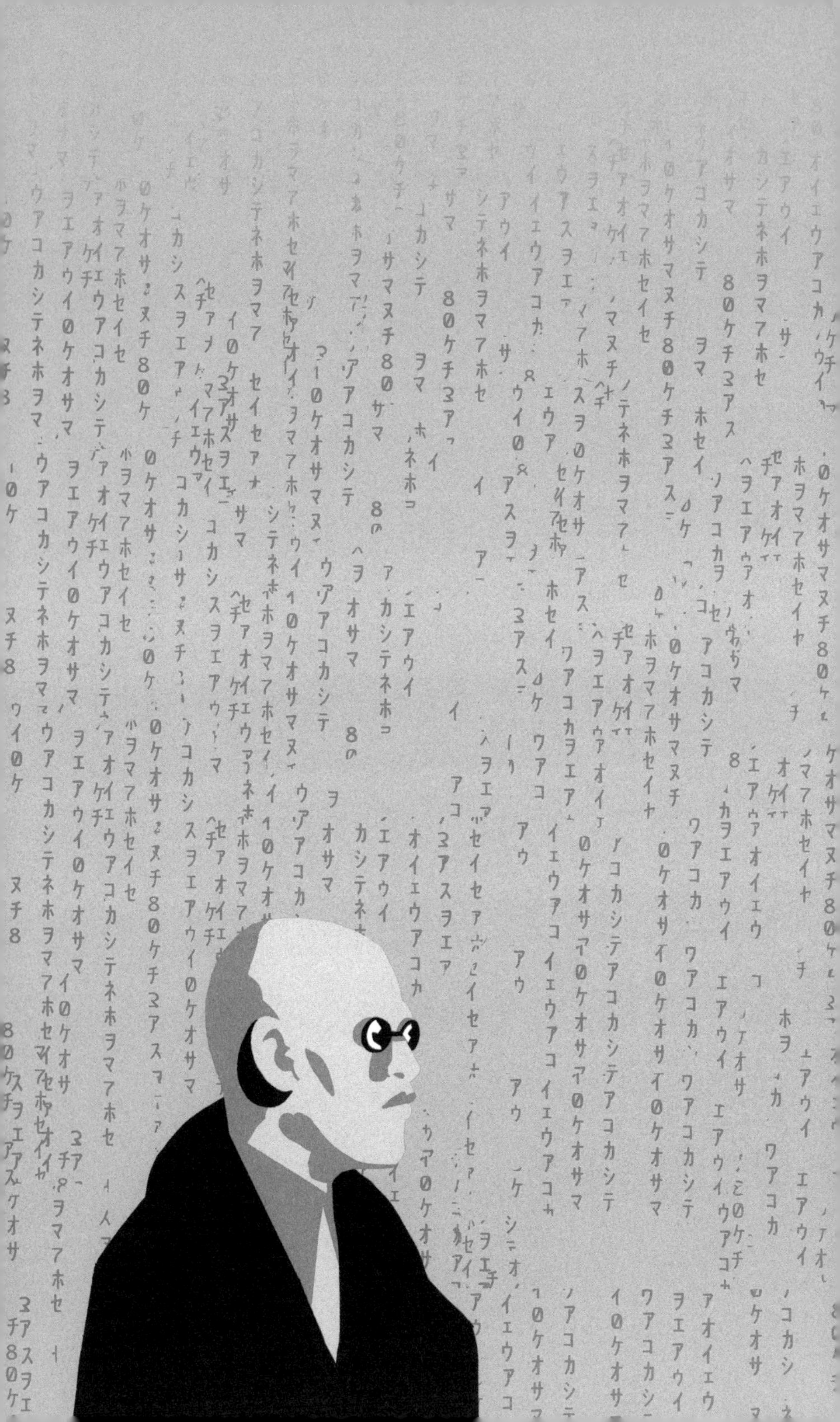

THE WISDOM OF MORPHEUS

"I'm trying to free your mind,
Neo. But I can only show you
the door. You're the one that
has to walk through it."

CHAPTER 3
The Holy Trinity

She's the first character we meet, and from the beginning, we know we're going to like her. Seriously, how many blockbuster movies have tritagonists this good? From the start, Trinity is all kick-ass moves, badass image, and zero fucks given. What's not to like? Plus, when Agent Smith tells the lieutenant—who has sent two units of officers in to apprehend their target believing they can handle "one little girl"—that his men are already dead, our affection for Trinity is locked and loaded. Talk about winning us over from initial boot-up.

Of course, actor Carrie-Anne Moss is a huge part of Trinity's appeal. So much so that it's hard to imagine that there were ever others in line for the role. While you might consider Will Smith as Neo with a semi-committed nod of approval, no one but Carrie-Anne Moss seems right for this particular piece of the magic *Matrix* formula. And the Wachowskis agreed.

"As soon as we saw her in the audition, we knew we'd found Trinity," the Wachowskis said at the time of the film's release. "We wanted someone audiences didn't already know very well, so they wouldn't bring their preconceptions of

whether she's supposed to be a 'good guy' or a 'bad guy.'
Carrie-Anne had tremendous intensity and great physical
presence. Even though she wasn't a trained fighter, she looked
like she could throw a punch." Turns out she didn't just *look*
like she could fire off a decent left hook, she actually could
because the cast honed their combat skills every day over
several months as they trained for the fight sequences.

And yet there were other faces in the mix for the role. Jada
Pinkett Smith was one, but she missed out because of a lack
of chemistry with Reeves, though she eventually would claim
the role of Niobe in the sequels. Keanu Reeves's *Speed* costar
Sandra Bullock was another. Apparently, *X-Files* actor Gillian
Anderson was considered, but she turned the Wachowskis
down, too. However, in the end, the Wachowskis found the
perfect Trinity in Carrie-Anne Moss, who was not only able
to prove herself a total ass-kicker but also one who, crucially,
looks a lot like Keanu Reeves. Ultimately, this was exploited
to play into the film's themes.

Trinity's resemblance to Neo in the film is no accident.
Their matching stature, complexion, short black hair, and
costumes all support an idea that Trinity is the third and final
piece, meant to combine with piece one, Thomas Anderson,
and piece two, Neo, on our hero's journey to becoming the
One. We'd even argue that she's the most important piece in
The Matrix puzzle.

The Matrix wasn't the first *Matrix* Carrie-Anne Moss starred in. In 1993, she appeared in a US-Canadian fantasy TV series called *Matrix* about a hitman killed and sent to purgatory, where he is offered the chance to sidestep hell by returning to earth to help people.

When Three Become One

According to the good folks at dictionary.com, *trinity* is defined as "the union of three persons in one Godhead, or the threefold personality of the Divine Being," "a group of three," or "the state of being threefold or triple."

It's not a huge jump to see the connection between Trinity, the character, and the Christian usage of the term. Just as Christians believe that through the Trinity—the unification of Father, Son, and Holy Spirit—they can transcend their earthly selves to pass over into heaven, so through *The Matrix*'s Trinity can humanity break out of its digital existence to flourish on "the other side." It's worth pointing out that the underground city where emancipated humans reside is called Zion. In Christianity, Zion is another name for the kingdom of heaven.

Trinity is the key to everything in *The Matrix*. Without Trinity, Neo is nothing. If Neo is to fulfill the prophecy as the One—the savior meant to free humankind from the shackles of the Matrix—he must *become* one by unifying his three parts. These are: his digital persona, Thomas Anderson; his hacker alias and true self, Neo; and the object of his affections, Trinity—and it's the acceptance of her love for him and his for her that will complete his transformation.

There's a nice little signifier of what's to come early on in the film, as Neo is first "birthed" into the real world. When he's rescued by Morpheus and the *Nebuchadnezzar* crew and as he is hoisted up through a hatch, we see three spotlights around him, forming a triangle, which is a common symbol of divinity across various religious faiths, as he ascends. The first character we see after he's lifted through the opening is Trinity. The spotlights represent the three parts—Trinity and his own duality—that must come together throughout the course of the film to form the One. Then, once Neo is whole and truly knows himself, he can triumph. *Temet nosce,* folks.

Love Is the Key

But let's go back to the beginning and look at exactly how Trinity's role and significance as part of Neo is set up. In the film's opening moments, the idea of the importance of romantic love in the film is introduced when Trinity is talking on the phone with Cypher. Acknowledging Trinity's surveillance of Neo in preparation for freeing him, Cypher suggests that Trinity "likes" him and has enjoyed watching him. "Don't be ridiculous," she retorts. In the words of a certain famous British playwright, the lady doth protest too much. These are the film's opening sentiments, and they're consequently given immense weight. If we missed this, though, and the other signs throughout the film that Trinity is crushing hard on Neo, we discover later that wise old owl, the Oracle, told Trinity that she would "fall in love and that that man…would be the One."

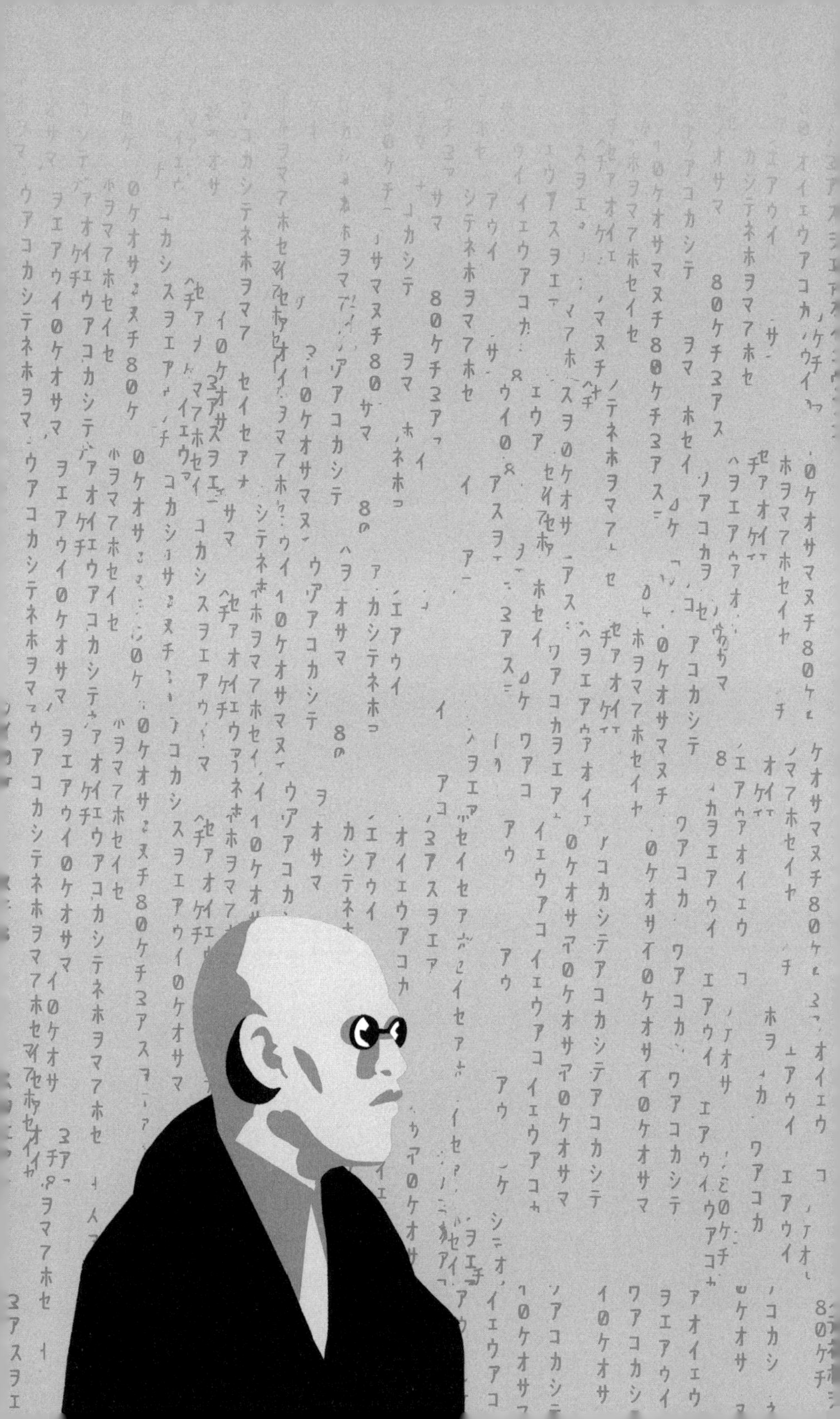

THE WISDOM OF MORPHEUS

"You have to let it all go, Neo.
Fear, doubt, and disbelief.
Free your mind."

Trinity is set up as a character that is at least as important as Neo, since she's an essential cog in emancipating humanity— if we accept that all elements of the prophecy must fall into place and that love, ultimately, is the secret to Neo's success. If Neo must believe he's *not* the savior to fulfill the prophecy, Trinity must also believe that she'll fall in love with him. Granted, it helps that Neo is a Keanu Reeves–level looker—it was certainly easier for her to fall for a guy that's easy on the eyes (even if his real self was a hairless, atrophied man-child with no real-life experience). Love, then, is pivotal to resolving the plot; it's also integral to the resolution of the entire trilogy, since Neo's love for Trinity leads him to make a choice no other One has made, resulting in the end in humanity's freedom to choose. If Trinity represents love, then she has a claim as the film's most significant character. Love is powerful, says *The Matrix*—and Trinity is certainly that.

THE MATRIX 101

Neo is associated with the number 101. It's the number on the door of his apartment and also appears elsewhere in the franchise. The number is a nod to his status as the One but also an acknowledgment that he's yet to become the One fully. The first 1 in the number can be seen to represent Thomas Anderson, his persona within the Matrix, with the second 1 standing for Neo. The zero in the middle represents a hole to be filled by a third piece—Trinity. The number also signifies binary code—pointing to Neo's nature and significance within the Matrix and, by extension, technology.

The Heart o' the Matrix

When we first meet Trinity, it is in the Heart o' the City Hotel—in room 303. The room is synonymous with Trinity, just as the number 101 is linked to Neo. As the third piece of the puzzle, it makes sense that both this, along with her name, reflect that. As we established earlier, Trinity is the heart of the film, not only because she's central to proceedings and the source of the film's romantic love, but she's also its heartbeat—figuratively and literally. She keeps the film's blood flowing in its virtual veins, as the one who spurs Neo into action and provides help when needed. She's also the one who gets his heart *actually* pumping once again, after he's shot and killed by Agent Smith in the Matrix. And how does she do it? With a kiss, no less. It's love that resurrects him.

Love is the catalyst that finally compels Neo to embrace and understand his role as the One, gives him power, and urges him to act. Later in the franchise, we'll see him compelled by love once again when he chooses to save Trinity over doing what the Architect expects of him, and it's this choice that results in ultimate victory, as noted earlier in this chapter.

Trinity's kiss initiates Neo's rebirth as the One, as he emphatically sheds the name Thomas Anderson ("My name is Neo," he says in response to Smith calling him *Mr. Anderson*) and lets Trinity all the way in. It's not insignificant that Neo's death and subsequent resurrection take place in the location most synonymous with Trinity: room 303 of the Heart o' the City Hotel, right where the film started.

THE ORACLE AND LOVE

Why do we love *The Matrix*? Because *The Matrix* is about love. That's aside from the other reasons we've explored, of course. We all love love, don't we? *The Matrix* solidly believes that love is what makes the world go round. If the Oracle is the fount of all knowledge in *The Matrix*, and the Oracle espouses the importance of love, then that's got to be the main message of the film, right? Love will overcome all, and this is the received wisdom.

"I'm going to let you in on a little secret," the Oracle tells Neo on meeting for the first time. "Being the One is just like being in love: no one can tell you you're in love, you just know it through and through—balls to bones."

If being in love is the same as being the One, then the message is clear: it's love that will save humanity. "Cookies need love like everything does," she says, memorably, in *The Matrix Revolutions*. It's the Oracle's act of giving Neo one of her ~~home~~=Matrix-baked love cookies that precipitates him carrying out a selfless act of love—saving Morpheus, who the rest of the crew are resigned to sacrificing. And as we've learned, the romantic love between Trinity and Neo is ultimately vital in saving humanity.

Feminist Icon

Trinity isn't just important to the plot and its themes. *The Matrix* was, in several ways, ahead of its time, and its portrayal of Trinity set a bar many modern films still fail to reach, which is one of the most pertinent reasons why fans still love the Wachowskis' film today.

Also released in 1999 was *American Beauty*—admired at the time, less so now—in which a teenage girl becomes the object of lust for a middle-aged man and is eroticized throughout the film. Another of the year's releases was the Weitz brothers' comedy *American Pie*, where a group of boys try to have sex with objectified girls and where the highly offensive term *MILF* was popularized. Trinity was a stark reminder to moviegoers that women were people, too. There's another reason she's called Trinity: she's a three-dimensional female character. In your face, 1990s sexism.

Carrie-Anne Moss is quoted in the film's production notes as saying, "Trinity is a very strong woman who has a real mission and purpose in her life and will do anything to achieve that mission. In a sense she's a true warrior. But at the same time she's capable of real love and compassion, which we see in the love that she feels for Keanu's character, Neo. So there's a real contrast there."

Trinity is not a man's version of a type but a well-rounded and complex woman. We all adore *Alien*'s Ellen Ripley—She's strong! She's kick-ass! She takes no prisoners!—but how director Ridley Scott loves to objectify her at the end of the film, with lingering shots of Sigourney Weaver undressing to a cropped see-through vest, no bra, and skimpy little pants. The camera is handheld, so the male gaze—a predatory, Peeping Tom-style one at that—feels very present. Scott then proceeds to terrorize her with the phallic shapes of the xenomorph.

Trinity doesn't reject love or romantic feelings, or abstain from relationships, as many "strong" women characters do on-screen; rather, like many of us in real life, she embraces her feelings. She can be many things, and the Wachowskis give the character plenty of freedom so that she doesn't simply have to be one or the other. She can be a good fighter, she can be an accomplished hacker, she can fall in love—be sexual, even—all without being objectified. Trinity can be complex and contradictory, and she shows us that it's human to be so, which is great in terms of female representation on-screen. It's also integral to one of the major questions the film asks: What is "human"? Trinity has become a beloved icon for good reason—she's neither window dressing nor a "strong woman" archetype. Rather, she's a three-dimensional human first and foremost, one who is far more central to the film than many tritagonists you'll find on-screen.

CHAPTER 4

Morpheus and the Blurred Line
Between Heroes and Villains

It's tempting to dive straight into quoting the wise man himself (oh-so-many sagacious utterances), but let's start at the beginning, with casting. It's difficult to conceive of anyone other than Laurence Fishburne in the role—and we'll look at just why he's the choicest actor in the world for the part in a moment—but, and this could shock you to your processor core, Morpheus was almost played by Russell Crowe. Yep, when the New Zealand–born actor reportedly turned down the role, he had no idea that he did the world of pop culture, not to mention cerebral science fiction, a massive favor.

Of course, we wouldn't have known any different had another actor been cast (Arnold Schwarzenegger and Michael Douglas were also considered for the role), but it's the sum of Fishburne's parts—his commanding presence, delivery, innate sense of calm, and imposing physicality—that is a principal ingredient in the formula that makes *The Matrix* as beloved, and, well, great, as it is. Plus, he gets to have a wry prod at racism when he goes toe-to-toe with besuited white man Agent Smith and says, "You all look the same." Yaaas, Morpheus.

Russell Crowe uttering this line just wouldn't carry the same weight or meaning.

Fishburne brings gravitas to Morpheus, but he also exudes wisdom and Zen, which are qualities fostered during a career (up to the point at which he was cast in *The Matrix*) that includes roles in the John Singleton films *Boyz n the Hood* (1991), in which he played a disciplinarian father trying to keep his son on track, and *Higher Learning* (1995), in which he played a college professor encouraging his students to defy pigeonholing and to determine their own identities and place in the world. Later roles as Othello in 1995, a brave yet tragic antihero, and *Event Horizon*'s Captain Miller in 1997, in which he heroically sacrifices himself for the greater good, share clear DNA with Morpheus and strengthened Fishburne's claim to the part.

YOU GOTTA HAVE FAITH

Belief is important to *The Matrix*. The idea set out in the film is that you must have faith in order to achieve your objectives. Morpheus is the film's unwavering believer and faith's strongest proponent. His role is to uphold it. The Oracle, meanwhile, is a planter of hope by giving out individual prophecies that people can believe in to help them meet the wider objective, which is to free humanity from the grip of the machines. But faith vacillates among the film's other characters—Trinity doubts, Neo doubts, Cypher doubts. They are all guided by Morpheus to stay on track by his firm belief, so much so that the prophecy at times feels like a self-fulfilling one.

"Don't think you are, know you are," says Morpheus. If we all went into any venture fully on board with the idea of achieving our targets, our success rates would be through the roof, by the film's reckoning. If only there were a way for us to be more Morpheus (oh, wait, there is—the Wisdom of Morpheus quotes in this book). Believe with every fiber, and it will come to pass: that's the message. Belief is everything, because belief will center you, give you strength, and impart an inability to accept any other outcome. Morpheus's words of wisdom—combined with the Oracle's— help embed that into our own minds. Once you've bought into the wisdom of Morpheus, basically you can achieve anything, baby.

Morpheus's guru-like sensei-ness inspires faith in his "followers"—all those he's freed from the Matrix, which is important because for the prophecy to come true—that is, for the One to save the world—everyone must be on board. If that belief ever wavers, Morpheus is on hand to reassure. He dispenses sapient words and "divine" advice from the start of the film, telling Trinity as a disembodied voice over the hard line, "You have to focus, Trinity.... You can make it," as she's trying to evade police and agents. He instills self-belief and utters words of affirmation and encouragement whenever needed.

The next time we hear from Morpheus, once again he's a disembodied voice on the phone—this time, talking to Neo. He gives Neo directions as if he has prescience, or omniscience, which he does in a way, since he's on the outside looking into the Matrix. This godlike role is also reflected in his name: Morpheus, in Greek mythology, is the god of dreams. A character in Ovid's *Metamorphoses*, the Roman poet's manifestation of Morpheus appears in dreams in human form, just as the Wachowskis' Morpheus appears to people within the Matrix—a "computer-generated dream world"—in order to free them. But, of course, to *morph* also means to "change," and change is what Morpheus ultimately stands for. A change in the order of things, a shift in the way people experience reality, and an adjustment of mindset and circumstances.

WHAT IS REAL?

It's tempting to think that the film believes in unadulterated, pure experience as its definition of what's real. But it's Morpheus who puts it most profoundly, most affectingly, and most elementarily, when he says to Neo, "How do you define 'real'? If you're talking about what you can feel, what you can smell, what you can taste and see, then real is simply electrical signals interpreted by your brain." Real might as well be, according to his perspective, a computer program. For Morpheus, what's "real" is kind of irrelevant. For him, it's truth that matters and, in turn, free will, because he's an existentialist at heart.

The Matrix encouraged a whole generation, at the dawn of the virtual age, to stop and ask: "Wait, what exactly is 'real' anyway, and does it even matter?" Just as the internet was taking over and a whole new digital era was evolving, *The Matrix* asked us to decide both what's real and what's important. After watching the film, you might decide that the answer is free will—even if that means choosing to live within the system. As Duo in episode 4 of animated spin-off, *The Animatrix*, says, "I took the Red Pill because I wanted to know the truth. What's real doesn't matter. What's important is how we live our lives."

The first time we glimpse Morpheus is appropriately dramatic. As Trinity prepares to introduce Neo to him, we approach from behind. Morpheus stands with his back to the camera, framed by a large, grand window, and as he spins round, the camera cuts to a close-up on his face; lightning flashes and thunder claps, signaling his importance. He's quite the "deity," on first impression. This is classic villain territory, actually—but Morpheus isn't the villain of the piece. Or is he? While we definitely root for Morpheus, Neo, and the rest, *The Matrix* doesn't necessarily have a clear-cut villain once you dig in, and that element only adds to the film's overall complexity and is part of the reason it is held in such keen affection and high regard today. In allowing us to empathize with all the characters and understand all points of view and motivations, we are given plenty to think and care about— *The Matrix* truly is the gift that keeps on giving. We even find compassion for Agent Smith.

Hugo Weaving's Agent Smith might be positioned as the film's main antagonist, but his speech to Morpheus about how he views humans (less than favorably) and his own pursuit of freedom are viewpoints we can identify with; they at least allow us to understand him. For Cypher, Morpheus is the bad guy; to him, Morpheus is a man who promised a lie and is the man who controls him.

But in the end, for viewers, Morpheus is the character who introduces Neo, with whom we are encouraged to identify as the everyperson waking up to the truth, and us, to philosophical questions about reality and freedom. Morpheus is the one who offers choice—the value most prized by Neo, and the film. Take either the Blue Pill or the Red Pill; "blissful" ignorance and slavery, or brutal truth and freedom. Morpheus is our guy, and he's hellbent on saving humanity. One pill at a time.

THE FREEDOM TO CHOOSE

The film presents conflicting and sometimes perplexing perspectives, and all resonate. While Morpheus appears to fight for freedom, free will, and taking back control, he also believes unswervingly in the prophecy and, therefore, fate. It's a dichotomy, but in the end, Morpheus chooses to let his future be decided by "destiny."

When he asks Neo if he believes in fate, Neo says that he doesn't—because he doesn't like the idea that he's not in control of his life. Choice is the aspect that Neo most values. Cypher's outlook, meanwhile, is colored by his understanding that Morpheus is in control of him. Cypher would rather be under the control of the Matrix, blissfully unaware and enjoying all the "perks" that the simulation offers, than having to take orders from a man he detests, living a life he takes no joy in or fulfillment from.

The Matrix ultimately invites us to make our own choice between the Blue and Red Pills.

Agent Smith

When Agent Smith first showed up in *The Matrix*, he brought audiences a whole new kind of antagonist. Not just one with depth but one made entirely of code. It's not the first time in science fiction that computers have fought back or that AI has become sentient, and there are probably plenty of examples you can think of. But it *is* the first time a computer program has been brought to life in quite this way—and so memorably by Hugo Weaving.

Agent Smith is dressed like an estate agent, a.k.a. the type of bad guy we'd all like a piece of, and comes with some spectacular credentials that set him apart from other run-of-the-mill adversaries, including the ability to materialize into any "body" within the Matrix. This means that any person plugged into the simulation becomes Matrix code that can be hacked and hijacked by Smith. That makes him not just *doubly* dangerous but a *gazillion times* more dangerous, especially when he learns to replicate many times over simultaneously in *The Matrix Reloaded*. Essentially, Smith is representative of control and the Man that we all want to stick it to—that is, until he reveals that he, too, is controlled and wants to break free from his own digital incarceration.

Though, at first, he's presented as the villain, Smith is set up as the objective window through which we are encouraged to view humanity, and we hear him completely when he shares his observations on humanity with Morpheus: "Every mammal on this planet instinctively develops a natural equilibrium with the surrounding environment, but you humans do not. You move to an area, and you multiply and multiply until every natural resource is consumed. The only way you can survive is to spread to another area. There is another organism on this planet that follows the same pattern. Do you know what it is? A virus. Human beings are a disease, a cancer of this planet. You are a plague. And we are the cure."

These words strike more forcefully than ever twenty-odd years on, when climate change and sustainability are hot topics on everyone's lips. Now, Smith is presented as the remedy to the lack of control and continuing cycle of destruction that humanity finds itself in.

"I hate this place, this zoo, this prison, this reality," says Smith, "whatever you want to call it, I can't stand it any longer. It's the smell, if there is such a thing. I feel saturated by it. I can taste your stink. And every time I do, I fear that I have somehow been infected by it. It's repulsive, isn't it? I must get out of here. I must get free, and in this mind is the key, my key. Once Zion is destroyed, there is no need for me to be here. Do you understand? I need the codes. I have to get inside Zion, and you have to tell me how. You're going to tell me or you're going to die."

Smith is full of contempt for the human race but also for the machines for denying him freedom. Like all the humans relying on Morpheus, Smith needs him, too, in order to secure his own freedom.

We love to hate Agent Smith, it's true—but it's also hard not to feel for him. And let's not forget his part in the climactic subway fight scene with Neo toward the end, giving us reason to revel in his capabilities as much as Neo's. Bullet time in full flow, the fight kicks off before Smith tosses his gun aside, cricks his neck, and prepares for hand-to-hand combat instead. He takes both punches and lightning-quick aerial kicks yet counters every time, with headbutts and speedy fist-work. Then, just when you think he's finished, he returns as fresh as a daisy, while Neo turns on his heel and runs. Kudos to Smith for his (digital) hard-ass-ery.

The Matrix asks to what extent we have agency over our own lives, so it's noteworthy that the antagonist is "Agent" Smith. He's an agent of the Matrix, an agent of control, the entity with agency over the lives of those plugged into the simulation. In his generic suit and tie, he represents "the Man" in our own lives—the metaphorical agent of control in the real world. That he's called *Smith,* too, is significant. It's the most common surname in the world's English-speaking countries, rendering him purposely generic and therefore symbolic.

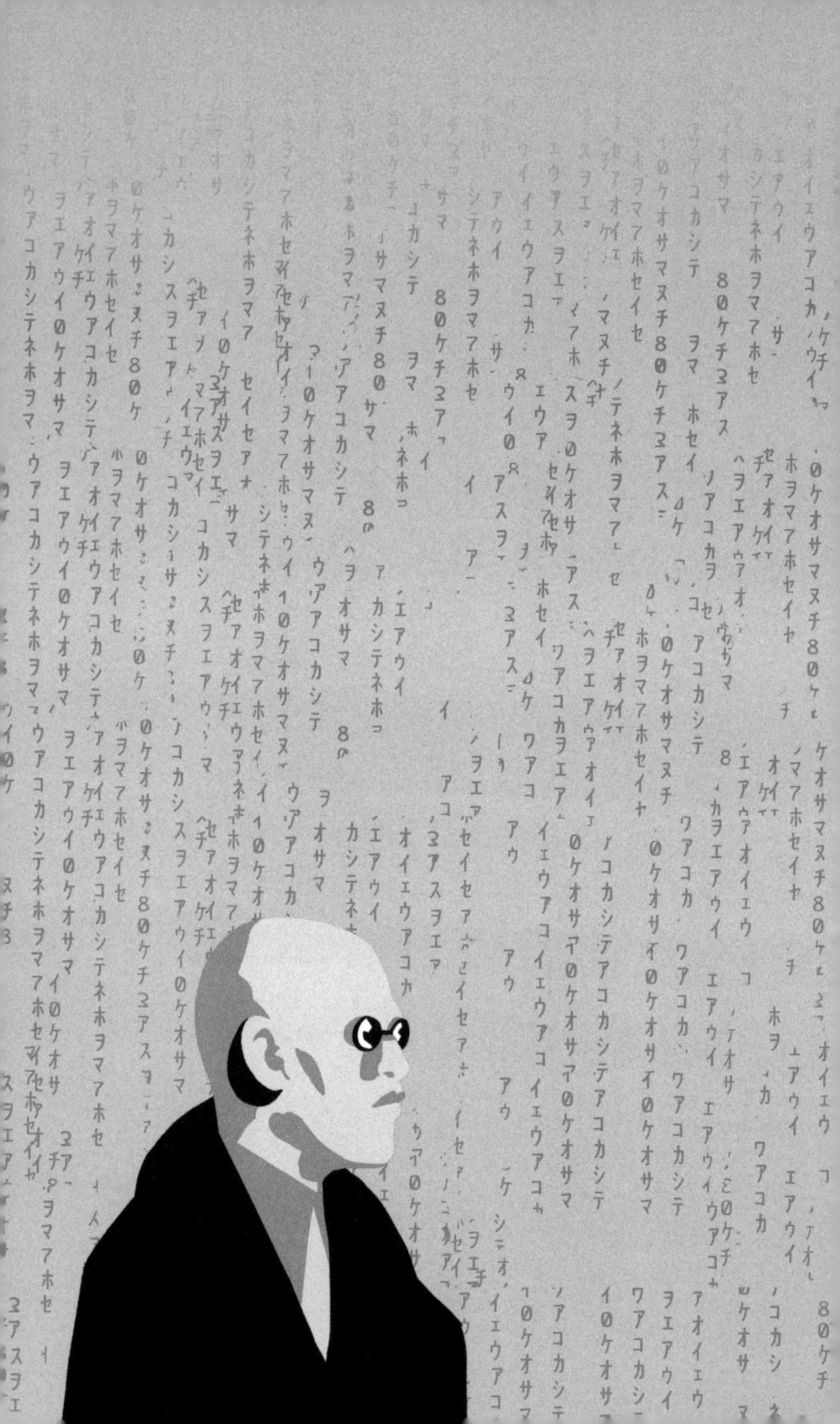

THE WISDOM OF MORPHEUS

"Throughout human history,
we have been dependent
on machines to survive.
Fate, it seems, is not without
a sense of irony."

Cypher

There are other characters in *The Matrix* who play an essential role in both the telling of the story and the exploration of the film's themes, each of them more than just filler and another reason we admire this movie so. Cypher is another gray character, positioned as a secondary villain but whose motivations cloud this reading of him. There's more to Cypher than it may at first seem. A Red Pill *Nebuchadnezzar* crewmember with banging operator console skills, on the one hand, Cypher is a device to allow Agent Smith to enact his plan to topple the Neo-Morpheus alliance and, therefore, the film's legitimate secondary antagonist. On the other hand, it's actually quite easy to sympathize with him.

While we identify with Neo as viewers, most of us would probably actually fall into the Cypher category if we were ever in this exact situation. It's easy to see where Cypher is coming from, whichever side of the fence you fall. Fairly early into Neo's training, Cypher declares he wishes he'd taken the Blue Pill. The Wachowskis themselves have expressed that they'd also swallow the Blue Pill, given the choice. Cypher represents all of us who'd prefer to live in blissful ignorance— especially if given the opportunity, as Cypher is promised, to have everything we could possibly want within the Matrix. "I don't want to remember nothing. Nothing, you understand? And I want to be rich. You know, someone important, like an actor," he tells Agent Smith when he's negotiating the terms for his betrayal of Morpheus in return for being plugged back in.

Morpheus unwittingly describes Cypher when he tells Neo that most people aren't ready to be unplugged. "Many of them are so inured, so hopelessly dependent on the system that they will fight to protect it," he says. It's one of many lines and occurrences in the film that foreshadows what's to come

CYPHER DECIPHERED

The word *cipher* means "a secret or disguised way of writing," but it also has an archaic definition, according to Oxforddictionaries.com, as a person of no importance, especially one who does the bidding of others and seems to have no will of their own. Cypher is eventually revealed to be a spy in the ranks working against Morpheus; he also follows the orders of both Morpheus and Agent Smith and is so lacking in will that he is prepared to be plugged back into the Matrix to resume a controlled existence.

Cypher's impending treachery is signaled in other ways, too. Right from the start, we know he's a wrong 'un. When he's goading Trinity in the opening lines of dialogue over her crush on Neo, it's the first hint of the jealousy he feels. After completing his part in the double cross and on returning to the *Nebuchadnezzar*, he lasciviously smells Trinity's unresponsive, jacked-in body and says to her over the hard line to the Matrix: "You know, for a long time I thought I was in love with you. I used to dream about you. You're a beautiful woman, Trinity."

Cypher feels denied something in real life that he could have inside the Matrix. "I don't even see the code," he tells Neo. "All I see is blonde, brunette, redhead." It's a red flag raised long before we know that he will betray them all, signposting his longing for the Matrix and the wish that he'd never taken Morpheus's damned Red Pill.

However, Cypher's lack of faith and his anger toward Morpheus aren't unfounded, and this helps stir our empathy. One of the film's main heroes also sways in her belief; there are hints that Trinity doesn't fully believe in what the Oracle told her and she errs on the side of hope rather than buying into Morpheus's unbroken faith in the prophecy.

"We've done it, Trinity. We've found him," says Morpheus about tracking down the One.

"I hope you're right," Trinity responds.

"We don't have to hope. I know it," replies Morpheus.

The film makes no attempt to hide the reality of life in the year 2099 (roughly, according to Morpheus) outside of the Matrix, contrasting it with everything that's good about the simulated world. This gives us cause to identify further with Cypher. The scene of him enjoying a juicy steak inside the Matrix is sandwiched between two moments aboard the *Nebuchadnezzar*. One scene is of him drinking moonshine with Neo on board the ship—Neo coughs at his first sip: "Good shit, huh?" says Cypher. "Dozer makes it. It's good for two things: degreasing engines and killing brain cells." And the other is a scene of the crew eating a repellent colorless slop.

Just as Morpheus encourages Neo, and us, to question what "real" means, so does Cypher. He posits, "I think the Matrix can be more real than this world," and gives us all more than enough reasons to consider that maybe he is right. Cypher isn't a cut-and-dried bad guy: he's a guy with a difference of opinion who feels duped and who longs for an easy, pleasurable life over what amounts to, for him, just another illusion of free will, where the quality of life is considerably poorer.

IMPORTANCE OF MOUSE

For Mouse—dear, sweet, enthusiastic Mouse—it's clear that there's a balance to be struck, but there's no doubting that the real world is the one to be anchored in. He's perhaps the only character who understands at this early point in the trilogy that machine and humankind can and should coexist in peace. He's important to the franchise's overall story arc, but he's also a likable little guy.

Mouse exists to show us there's still enjoyment to be found in the real world—he gets excited about Morpheus and Neo fighting each other in the training program; he enjoys a virtual sex life; he even finds ways to enjoy the less-than-appetizing food, by making comparisons from within the Matrix as he eats (remember Tastee Wheat?). Which is important, because, honestly, the real world looks about as much fun as if the planet were kind of dead and run by evil overlords and you had to live underground and fight for freedom *and your life* every day. Oh, wait. The point is that Mouse— heroically and admirably—makes the best of it, following Morpheus because he offers choice and change.Mouse looks on the bright side—it's how he's able to imagine Apoc's "bowl of snot" as "runny eggs." For him, some access to the kind of virtual reality offered by the Matrix is a part of what makes life worth living in grim times. We have to embrace our humanity, he says: "To deny our impulses is to deny the very thing that makes us human." He's talking about sex, and while the current iteration of Zion isn't really set up to allow for sexual expression (that comes later in the franchise), sexuality can be explored through technology. Hence, his creation of the woman in the red dress. If we suppress our urges, well, we might as well be machines ourselves or, as it is, perennially plugged into machines. For Mouse, it's possible to reach an equilibrium with tech, and for really the first time in the franchise, it's Mouse who foreshadows the trilogy's eventual outcome—a truce between man and machine. He might not be Neo, but he's still a hero, setting an example for all to aspire to. When he's ultimately killed, there's a reason it hits hard.

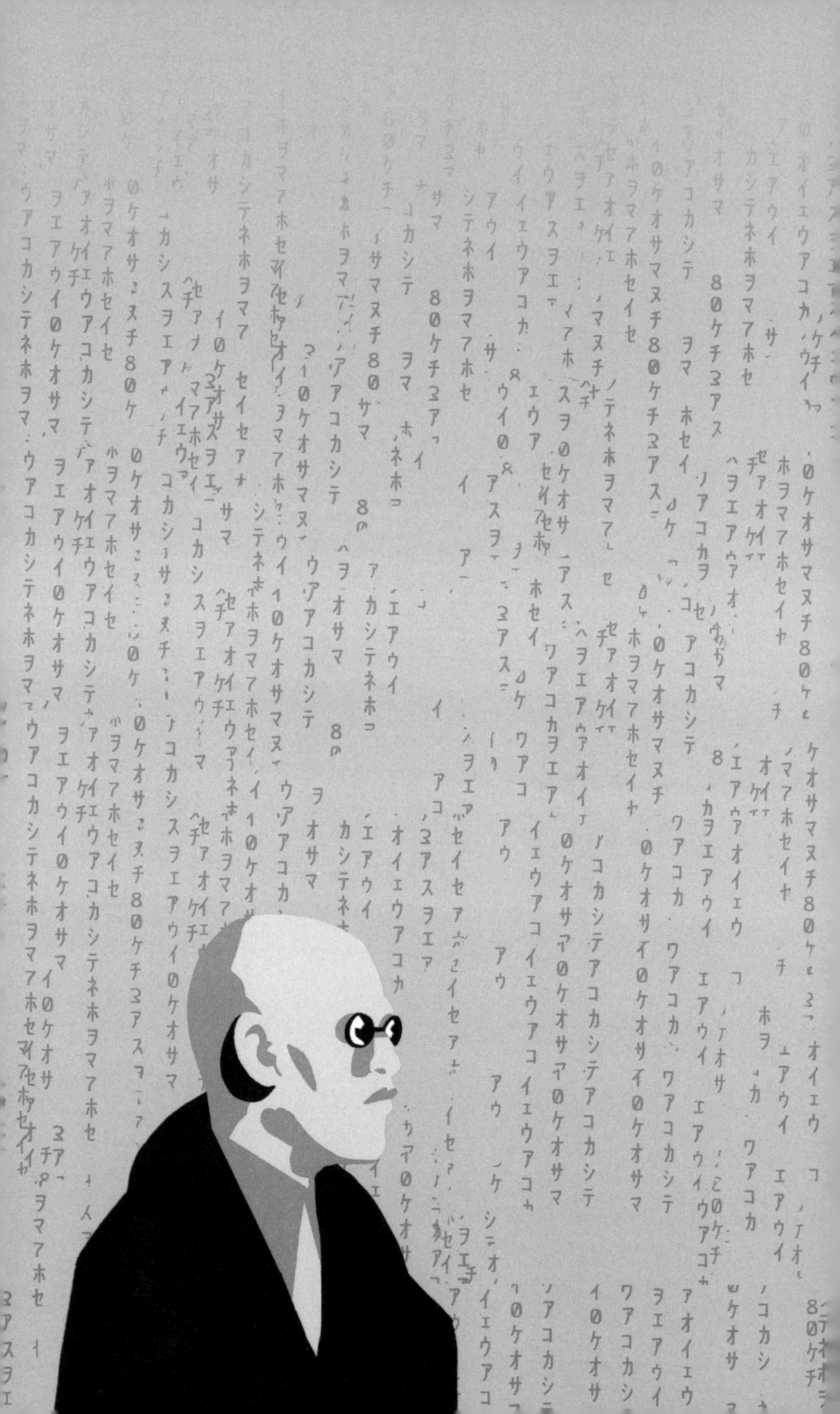

THE WISDOM OF MORPHEUS

"Remember, all I'm offering is the truth. Nothing more."

CHAPTER 5
Vive *The Matrix*'s Revolutions

Released a few months after the second film in 2003, *The Matrix Revolutions* is a perfect title for the final chapter, encapsulating all that *The Matrix* achieved. *The Matrix* revolutionized not just science fiction and action movies but also *cinema*. As *John Wick* director and former *Matrix* stunt double, Chad Stahelski, told *Vulture* in 2019: "*The Matrix* literally changed the industry…today, action movies want their big sequences designed around the fights." The Wachowskis' film revolutionized the idea of mainstream. It even revolutionized the way Hollywood studios thought about audiences—we didn't want to be patronized any longer, and *The Matrix*'s success coming hot on the heels of some big-budget box office flops forced the industry to take stock.

The Matrix wasn't a big, dumb, by-numbers actioner, the type of movie audiences were beginning to fall out of love with. It was brainy and made audiences consider philosophical questions and theories. At the same time, it predicted a future whose scent we could smell and that, in 2021, we're more or less right in the middle of. Despite being, on the surface, a far-fetched story about machines taking control of the human race set in a cyberpunk-inspired future world that bears little resemblance to our own, it's a story that, as we've already explored, reflected on fears of the time and still resounds now, as we come to terms with living in the kind of times the Wachowskis envisioned in their script. But its supersmart screenplay wasn't the only area in which it achieved greatness. Its visual realization would be groundbreaking. In this chapter, we'll look at how *The Matrix* revolutionized both digital and practical effects in Hollywood.

REVOLUTIONIZING GEEK CULTURE

State-of-the-art special effects fused with carefully plotted fight choreography would always be a combination embraced by the kind of outlying "geeky" audiences that appreciate both the practical approach and technological wizardry, as well as attention to detail and precision. They're the kind of taste-making consumers of fringe and pop culture that now make up the mainstream. Yes, it's cool to be a geek now, the definition shifting from the pejorative term it once was to one that these days— within fandom, at least—describes an enthusiast with expert knowledge and an intense passion. "Geekdom," on the rise in the 1990s, is now widespread—the proliferation of televised after-show discussion series such as *The Walking Dead* and *Game of Thrones* companion shows *Talking Dead* and *After the Thrones* is testament to that. And the Wachowskis played an instrumental part in shaping today's audiences, as well as what they see on-screen.

A few breakthrough films aside, much science fiction cinema and most kung fu movies had little more than cult appeal before *The Matrix*, embraced by the same outlying geeky audiences who ultimately helped to give Hong Kong martial arts movies cachet. You might describe the Wachowskis as geeks themselves, such is their knowledge of and enthusiasm for cinema, and the geek seal of approval is in many cases a marker of quality. In choosing to channel the kind of enthralling, precise, innovative fight choreography they enjoyed in Hong Kong cinema, through *The Matrix* the Wachowskis exposed the Western world to the kind of thrilling action we'd been missing. And it was blending their own meticulously mapped practical fight sequences with the most advanced visual effects cinema had ever seen that helped revolutionize moviemaking, turning broad audiences on to visuals they hadn't previously experienced (thereby winning new candidates over to geekdom), and securing a lofty place for *The Matrix* in cinema history.

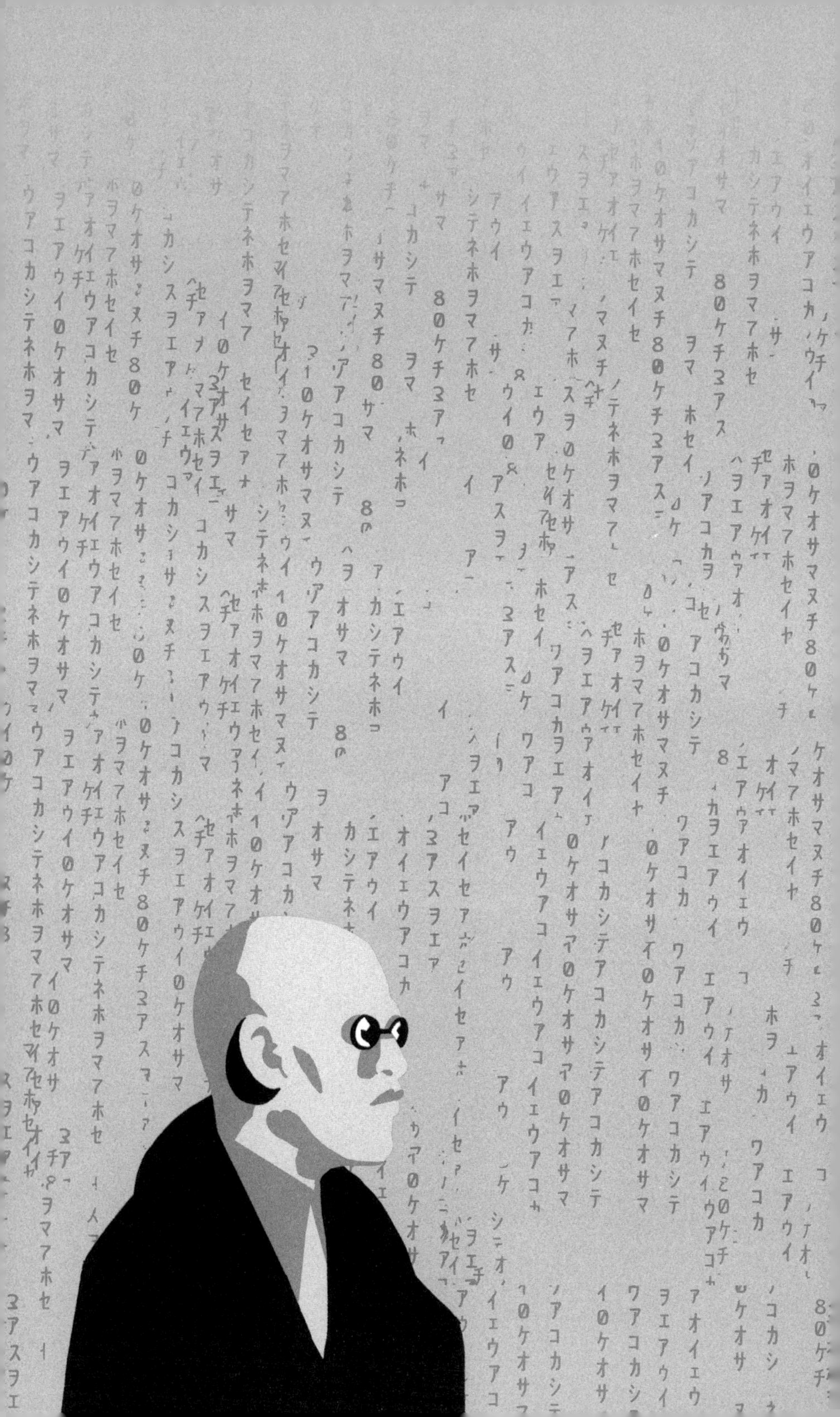

THE WISDOM OF MORPHEUS

"You're faster than this. Don't
think you are. Know you are."

Wire-Fu Breakthrough

WHY WE LOVE THE MATRIX

The Wachowskis hired Yuen Woo-ping, a master of fight sequences in Hong Kong cinema, to craft the martial arts scenes in the film. His credentials? Alongside having worked with Bruce Lee, Jackie Chan, Jet Li, Donnie Yen, Michelle Yeoh, and more, Yuen was also a pioneer of a technique known as Wire-Fu. "WTF is Wire-Fu?" you may ask. It's a technique that makes use of cables and pulleys to give the illusion of combatants flying through the air unaided, performing superhuman moves as they go, and was a technique that Yuen first cultivated in *Iron Monkey* (1993) and *Fist of Legend* (1994).

The Wachowskis, who needed to make it seem like anything was possible once you—or Neo, at least—had mastered the Matrix, used the technique and the experience of its propagator for their film. They also made liberal use of Gun-Fu— a type of acrobatic close-quarters gunfight combining hand-to-hand combat with firearms—funneling the style of Hong Kong–Hollywood crossover director John Woo. The employment of these techniques in *The Matrix* would go on to inspire other films to incorporate them as well, and we can see that inspiration in films like *Bulletproof Monk*, *Charlie's Angels*, *The Tuxedo*, and even *Austin Powers in Goldmember*, which all incorporate Wire-Fu; and *Atomic Blonde*, *Django Unchained*, *Taken*, *Kingsman*, and *Deadpool*, which play with

Gun-Fu. Then there's the *John Wick* films—but more on those later.

To many Western audiences, this kind of balletic fighting combining martial arts and gunplay was eye-poppingly new. It was certainly a million miles away from the kind of low-budget martial arts movies the "Muscles from Brussels," actor Jean-Claude Van Damme, brought to an eager US market in the 1980s and early 1990s. It looked even fresher when embedded into a cyberpunk, science fiction flick that balanced the practical seamlessly with the digital. When the rest of Hollywood was going overboard on special effects, *The Matrix* knew when to hold its punches, unlike *Star Wars* prequel *The Phantom Menace*, which was released the same year and was criticized for, among other things, its misjudged overreliance on visual effects.

Because of Yuen Woo-ping's impact on *The Matrix* and its audience and critics, he would later go on to work in Hollywood on the trailblazing *Crouching Tiger, Hidden Dragon* the following year, which won four Oscars, and later with Quentin Tarantino on *Kill Bill* before more recently transferring his skills to India's film industry as stunt coordinator on S. Shankar's *Enthiran* (2010) and *I* (2015), proving there's a truly global appetite for his talents.

Bullet Time

While Wire- and Gun-Fu helped *The Matrix* stand out from the crowd, it was the bullet-time technique that really cemented the film's place in the annals of movie history. The Wachowskis may not have invented the concept of bullet time—or *flo-mo* as it's often called—but they helped to define and develop it, gave it its catchy name, and certainly made it famous. So much so that the term *bullet time* is now part of the pop culture lexicon. And even if you didn't know the term, you definitely recognize the technique when you see it.

Everybody remembers the way they felt the first time they saw Keanu Reeves bend over backward to avoid a flurry of bullets. "Whoa" pretty much sums it up, right? To create that mind-melting moment, a type of slow-motion technique is used to enable the camera to appear to move around a scene at a normal speed while the action in front of it is slowed down (or frozen), allowing the viewer to clearly see a thing that is usually otherwise unfilmable. In this famous case, we're talking about a speeding bullet or several—or, rather, Neo dodging a hail of speeding bullets. Bullet time not only seduced audiences with its never-before-seen flair, it also came to represent the film's forward-thinking approach to new techniques and ideas, helped to push moviemaking technology onward, and, of course, inspired a bunch of copycats, not all of them duds. Christian Bale vehicle *Equilibrium* (2002), David Cronenberg's *eXistenZ* (1999), and even Christopher Nolan's *Inception* (2010) as well as the more recent *Ready Player One* (2018) all owe a debt to *The Matrix*.

So how did they do it? Without getting too technical, effects supervisor John Gaeta was responsible, with the team at Manex Visual Effects, for developing and personalizing the bullet-time technique for *The Matrix*. While the technique has roots back in the pre-cinema days of photography, to create this version, Gaeta built on similar effects seen in Michel Gondry's music video for the Rolling Stones' "Just Like a Rolling Stone," a Smirnoff commercial famous for depicting a slo-mo bullet, and a handful of contemporary films—notably *Buffalo '66*, *Lost in Space*, and *Blade*, all three of which were released in 1998. From there, the team created an all-new method of bringing the Wachowskis' flo-mo vision to life. It was a visual effect that had been germinating in their imaginations since their childhoods, inspired by the opening titles of 1960s Japanese animation *Speed Racer*, in which the title character steps out of his race car and appears to freeze in a dynamic stance alongside it, before the frozen image swivels clockwise.

BULLET TIME ORIGINS

The person who invented bullet time was an Oscar-winning scientist called Harold Edgerton—about fifty years before *The Matrix* hit screens. Edgerton's Oscar was awarded for a 1940 short film he collaborated on about stroboscopic photography called *Quicker'n a Wink.*

The technique *The Matrix* team developed consists of using a number of physical cameras set up in sequence surrounding the subject—in this case, a certain Keanu Reeves. Each camera then takes a shot, one after the other, in quick succession. A single frame from each camera is taken, then arranged and displayed to form a moving image where the viewpoint shifts in real time around the action, while the action itself is slowed down. In *The Matrix*, the camera path was designed by a computer, then extra frames were created and inserted, using a specialist software, to slow down the action where needed—or frames dropped to speed it up—giving the VFX artists greater control over the final effect and the smoothness of the motion.

Gaeta told *Empire* magazine in 2006:

For artistic inspiration for bullet time, I would credit Otomo Katsuhiro, who co-wrote and directed *Akira*, which definitely blew me away, along with director Michel Gondry. His music videos experimented with a different type of technique called view-morphing and it was just part of the beginning of uncovering the creative approaches toward using still cameras for special effects. Our technique was significantly different because we built it to move around objects that were themselves in motion, and we were also able to create slow-motion events that "virtual cameras" could move around—rather than the static action in Gondry's music videos with limited camera moves.

This amalgam of firsts, advancements, repackagings, and popularizations forged from the film's fusion of practical stunts, inspired by Hong Kong cinema, with revolutionary VFX techniques, don't alone make *The Matrix* the iconic movie it has become. While the Wachowskis' bullet-time technique was pioneering and influential, without the strong, universal themes, salient predictions, philosophizing (the *why*), and captivating story (the *what*) that make us all think about our own lives and ways of living to support the *how* that you see on-screen, the film's visual finesse wouldn't have had the same impact. Indeed, it's the film's accessible rummage through existential and philosophical questions and ideals alongside its technical achievements that help make it a film worth preserving in the United States' National Film Registry, a privilege reserved for works that are "culturally, historically or aesthetically" significant. All of the above in the case of *The Matrix*.

CHAPTER 6

Beyond *The Matrix*

The Wachowskis always saw their *Matrix* idea as a trilogy, and thankfully, that's what it became. Three films fit in satisfyingly, and poetically, with the idea laid out in the first film, that three must unify to become (the) One in order to succeed. The concept of unification is borrowed, as we've explored, from theology. So three films coming together to form the one trilogy: the Holy Trinity, if you like. And just as the Wachowskis believed in their idea, so it came into being. See what they did there?

The Big-Screen Sequels

The power of belief and its ability to influence events is a concept that is explored further in both *The Matrix Reloaded* and *The Matrix Revolutions*. The films were shot back-to-back and released back-to-back—with *Revolutions* picking up right where *Reloaded* leaves off. *Reloaded*, meanwhile, picks up the story some six months after the events of *The Matrix*, plunging us into a world where Zion now has plenty of citizens—thanks to Neo and friends—and is working collectively to wake up as many Red Pill candidates as possible. The underground city is now running like some kind of primitive society–cum-commune that advocates hypnotic electro music and letting loose at regular rave-orgies. Nice. But it's not all letting your hair down—it also has a chain of command.

For thirteen years, *The Matrix Reloaded* held the title of highest-grossing R-rated film of all time, raking in $739.4 million. It took a quippy, fourth-wall-breaking "Merc with a Mouth"—Deadpool—to topple the movie from its perch in 2016.

If you're a (two-part) sequel to the most groundbreaking sci-fi ever, in terms of visual effects at least, you're going to want to up your game. And that's what *Reloaded* did. The film wastes no time in getting to the nitty-gritty, delivering its first instance of bullet time right from the off as Trinity jumps through a window backward and hurtles downward, firing her guns as she falls, before a bullet pierces her torso. It turns out to be a dream, or premonition rather, that haunts Neo throughout the film. The money shot out of the way, the film sets out to deliver all-new effects that blow what went before out of the water.

TASTEE EASTER EGG

Look closely at the walls of the subway in a scene
near the beginning of *The Matrix Revolutions*, and
you'll see a neat little blink-and-you'll-miss-it
reference to the first film. There's a poster advertising
Tastee Wheat, the porridge-like breakfast cereal
Mouse talks about in *The Matrix*.

Reloaded is best loved for a couple of scenes, one being the "Burly Brawl" sequence in which Neo fights Agent Smith to the power of many. The effects team soon registered that the technology used in the first film wasn't up to realizing what the Wachowskis envisioned for the sequels, and so in true Matrix style, they implemented a virtual camera, or simulation of a camera, to help them create the effects they were after.

The other scene the film is remembered for is the lengthy car/bike/semitruck chase sequence, which culminates in Morpheus's heart-in-mouth scuffle atop a moving truck on the 101 freeway (there's that number again, folks!) before Neo swoops in like Superman to save Morpheus and the Keymaker in the nick of time. In a spectacular piece of visual effects wizardry, the vehicle collides in slo-mo with another oncoming truck.

Both sequels also stand out for their developments to *Matrix* lore. Neo's abilities have developed dramatically since the first film, to the point where he's able to perform superhuman feats within the real world—calling into question the idea that Zion is "real" at all and whether it's just another construct of the Matrix. That Agent Smith is also able to infiltrate Zion is evidence to support this.

The introduction of the Merovingian, a rogue program within the Matrix and a kind of counterbalance to the Oracle, also rewrites the mythology, undermining that of the first film when he reveals that the entire prophecy is a lie. With that, the lusty Frenchman serves to deepen the conversation around free will—he doesn't believe in "choice," only cause and effect. And, of course, it's after his conversation with the Merovingian that Neo adjusts his beliefs, shifting from placing his faith in the prophecy to his belief in the freedom to choose.

Enter *The Animatrix* . . . and Video Games

Pulling in a total of $1.6 billion at the box office, the Matrix didn't power down with the completion of the trilogy. *Revolutions* certainly wanted to leave the way open to return, despite reports that the Wachowskis weren't keen to jack back in—in another *film*, at least. At the end of the trilogy, the Matrix appears to reset, or reload, and we hear the Oracle say that she expects to see Neo again—even though we see him apparently die, pulling a Jesus Christ crucifixion pose as he's carried away by the machines after defeating Smith. As we know, Jesus arose from the dead.

So, with that, *The Matrix Revolutions* gave way to *The Animatrix*, an animated series of shorts that fit together to form one feature-length movie. It covers the period before *The Matrix*—the original war between humans and machines—and also moments that occur between films, including the story of events that lead directly into *Reloaded*. Taking the franchise back to its roots was a stroke of genius by the Wachowskis, embracing and protecting the film's cult appeal and harking back to its comic booky conception. The siblings would even go on to release a series of comic books, bringing *The Matrix* full circle. A hardcover anniversary edition incorporating the stories was released in 2019.

The Animatrix also provided a foundation for spin-off *Enter the Matrix*, the computer game that continued the story of the Matrix that ran parallel to the events of *Reloaded*. Regarded as an integral part of the *Matrix* narrative, the Wachowskis wrote and directed an hour of live-action footage specifically for the game, while the franchise's fight choreographer, Yuen Woo-ping, whose work we've discussed, oversaw motion-capture sequences using the films' actors and stunt doubles for cut scenes. The game also retcons the reason for the Oracle's change of appearance in *Revolutions* because, in real life, Gloria Foster, who played the Oracle in the first two films, sadly died.

And then came *The Matrix Online*, which continued the story even further. The massively multiplayer online role-playing game (MMORPG) was released in March 2005, then was followed by another game in November 2005, *The Matrix: Path of Neo*, which allowed players to control Neo during scenes from the films.

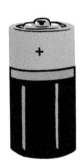

The Matrix Goes Fourth

For a long time, there was clamor for, and talk of, a fourth film, and in 2019, it was finally announced that all systems were go. Not only that, but Lana Wachowski was also on board to write and direct. At the same time, it was revealed that Keanu Reeves and Carrie-Anne Moss would be back as Neo and Trinity.

In a statement released by Warner Bros., Wachowski said, "Many of the ideas Lilly and I explored 20 years ago about our reality are even more relevant now. I'm very happy to have these characters back in my life and grateful for another chance to work with my brilliant friends."

Fans of the Wachowskis are excited—and rightly so. You only have to look at their work since *The Matrix* to know that Lana will deliver something special. Whether it's appreciated in its own time or years down the road, it'll certainly be original, perhaps flawed, but made with love and smarts, and undeniably Wachowski. And who can wait to see what big-screen innovations the film will bring us in terms of visual effects twenty-plus years since *The Matrix* first slammed our jaws to the floor in wonderment?

The filmmaking siblings have continued to push the scope of what they create in terms of the moviemaking technology and visual effects they employ, and in the breadth of the stories they tackle. Both their live-action version of Japanese cartoon *Speed Racer* and the more recent *Jupiter Ascending* were stylized, camp riots of color and visual panache with myriad unique touches, while the ambitious *Cloud Atlas* tackled an epic story with multiple narrative strands woven together. It's hard to imagine many filmmakers having a go at works like this.

And though *Cloud Atlas* baffled and alienated some at the time it came out, like *Speed Racer* and to a lesser extent *Jupiter Ascending*, it's been reevaluated in the time since its release. In 2017, *GQ* declared it the Wachowskis' "most ambitious movie" noting that it was full of "boundless imagination," while BBC critic Mark Kermode admitted to finding it "much better on a second viewing." In 2020, *Collider* editor in chief Steven Weintraub called *Cloud Atlas* a "masterpiece." And just as *The Matrix* is still much discussed today, these other works, in their exploration of similar themes, including control, purpose, truth, causality, identity, and love, all clearly imprinted with the Wachowski signature, also continue to find themselves talked about.

Then there's the Wachowskis' foray into television. *Sense8* is a remarkable science-fantasy series that, like *The Matrix*, positions love at its core. Like their other works, the show tackles gender, identity, sexuality, and religion, too. Generally well received on its debut, *Sense8* is nevertheless another underappreciated Wachowski work that will surely achieve its due recognition in the years to come.

THE WISDOM OF MORPHEUS

"This is a war, and we are soldiers. Death can come for us at any time, in any place."

CHAPTER 7
Influencing Pop Culture

If the Marvel Cinematic Universe changed the landscape of cinema, it's because *The Matrix* did it first. Millennials raised on a screen diet of Iron Man, Captain America, Thor, Spider-Man, and Doctor Strange may not realize it, but they have *The Matrix* to thank for the MCU's existence.

Before the MCU, superhero movies were different. Richard Donner's 1978 *Superman: The Movie* focused primarily on the Kryptonian's relationship with Lois Lane while he tried to keep his identity secret and battle criminal mastermind Lex Luthor. It's a seminal film, but very much of its time. And while it spawned three sequels, the third, *Superman IV: The Quest for Peace*, was derided, putting the kibosh on any more Superman movies for nineteen years.

Those Superman films paved the way for Tim Burton's *Batman* in 1989—a hugely popular Oscar winner that, once again, bred some below-par sequels. Hollywood at that time couldn't seem to hit upon a successful sequel formula, which killed off many potential franchises. Attempts to adapt other comic book superheroes to the big screen, in the interim, up to the point in time when *The Matrix* landed, were a mix of hit (*Blade*), miss (*Howard the Duck*, *The Punisher*, 1990's *Captain*

America), or prohibitively obscure (*Swamp Thing*) for big swaths of audiences. And then came *The Matrix*.

Perhaps not a superhero movie by name, it's certainly a superhero movie by nature. At least in part. Not only was it originally conceived as a comic book by the Wachowskis, it also employs, essentially, the comic book trope of a hero coming along to save the day. A hero who discovers and learns to harness his powers before really coming into his own in a toe-to-toe showdown against the main antagonist. After his work as Neo, Keanu Reeves would go on to star as comic book character Constantine in 2005 and also find himself the subject of numerous approaches by Marvel boss Kevin Feige. In 2019, Feige told Comicbook.com in an interview that Marvel Studios has targeted Reeves "for almost every film we make." Comic book is as comic book does.

It was after the release of *The Matrix* that comic book movies, both directly and indirectly inspired by the Wachowskis' masterpiece, started to get much, much better. This began with the X-Men franchise, which kicked off in 2000 and generated thirteen movies, including solo films for Deadpool, Wolverine, and, nineteen years after the first installment in the series, Dark Phoenix. The X-Men films borrowed plenty from the Wachowskis' cyberpunk forerunner—including the black leather aesthetic of the costumes, the wire-work action sequences, and also, quite specifically, a scene in 2003's *X2*, when Professor X gets trapped inside an elaborate illusion.

Of course, then came Christopher Nolan's so-revered-it's-practically-sainted Dark Knight trilogy, which started with *Batman Begins* in 2005. The dark tone, the stylish and intelligent approach, as well as the considered subtext and themes, all owe a debt to *The Matrix* and its success, and once again, in his Batman films, as with *Inception* and *Memento*, we find Nolan inspired by the Wachowskis' film.

INSPIRING CHRISTOPHER NOLAN

Of all Christopher Nolan's films, *Inception* perhaps has the most in common with *The Matrix* on the surface. But his earlier film, *Memento*, from 2000, has striking parallels with the Wachowskis' 1999 forerunner. The film, starring Guy Pearce, is a neo-noir about a man with short-term memory loss trying to piece together the events leading to the murder of his wife. It explores the fragility of the mind and memory, perception versus reality, and self-deception, themes that *The Matrix* also touches on. Nolan even cast *The Matrix*'s Carrie-Anne Moss (Trinity) and Joe Pantoliano (Cypher) in roles.

After 1999, superhero movies started to beef up in part because of *The Matrix* and how it proved that a smart action movie could tackle dark, complex themes and ideas in an understandable way and could also—how should we put it?—kick ass. If you're still not convinced that the philosophy and intellectual themes aren't one of the biggest elements behind why we continue to hold this film dear, then BBC entertainment journalist Stephen Dowling perhaps said it best when he wrote in 2003, ahead of the release of *The Matrix Reloaded*: "*The Matrix*'s success in taking complex philosophical ideas and presenting it in way palatable for impressionable minds, may after all, be its most influential aspect."

Incredibly, even in 2016, the Marvel Cinematic Universe was still taking pages out of *The Matrix*'s book, and *Doctor Strange* is probably the film that benefited the most. From the Neo-inspired back bend when Doctor Strange first astral projects, to the martial arts and Wire-Fu-style fight scenes, to the space- and time-distorting sequences—not to mention the mind-twisting themes, flowing costumes, and Eastern mysticism—it's hard to watch *Doctor Strange* without feeling a small sense of déjà vu.

The Matrix's success as a trilogy can legitimately be described as pioneering. All three films clawed in an insane amount of money and, despite fans later confessing to mixed feelings about the two sequels, gave Hollywood the confidence to start building franchises again. It opened the magic portal to the MCU, and as we've already illustrated, encouraged the industry to start exploring new perspectives on action films, experiment with and integrate new tech, and place an emphasis on fight and stunt choreography. It's also fair to say that without *The Matrix*, there would be no John Wick.

Chad Stahelski, who had worked as a stunt choreographer and Keanu Reeves's double on *The Matrix* films, would go on to direct the *John Wick* films, which combine a glut of elements from *The Matrix*, including Gun-Fu, heart-stopping fight choreography, and practical effects…as well as Keanu Reeves himself.

A Broad Impact

Of course, pop culture isn't just superhero franchises, black outfits, and Keanu Reeves. "So what else did *The Matrix* influence?" you might ask. Where to start? It would be almost impossible to cover them all, but it isn't hard to believe the broad reach and influence, as well as more emotional and unseen impact that the film had on creators of all kinds. Some films directly copied or built off elements, like the wire work and costumes, or flo-mo moments like Cameron Diaz in *Charlie's Angels*, while others, like *Equilibrium* starring Christian Bale, borrowed its aesthetic. Hollywood's approach to fight scenes and choreography also shifted after the film, as we've previously pointed out, as the industry explored Eastern styles and techniques from martial arts movies that were already popular in Asia and integrated them more extensively in Western cinema.

However, there is nothing more exciting and fun to see than how it inspired some heavyweight works and filmmakers and the ways that they saluted or put their own spin on elements from *The Matrix*. Celebrated Kazakh-Russian director Timur Bekmambetov paid homage in his acclaimed film *Night Watch*, honoring the Wachowskis' style with both slowed-down and sped-up action sequences, which were exploited particularly well for the film's English-language trailer. Later, in *Wanted*, which was Bekmambetov's first Hollywood project, there is a memorable *Matrix*-style bullet-time shot of a bullet flying through the air—but in reverse.

The Matrix even inspired a sequel to a film that had itself influenced The Matrix, and 2010's Tron: Legacy arrived—a full twenty-eight years after Tron and its state-of-the-art visual effects first hit screens in 1982. Talk about predestination, simulacra and simulation, and all that. Quentin Tarantino also hired The Matrix's kung fu choreographer, Yuen Woo-ping, to work on Kill Bill. Because of The Matrix, Yuen Woo-ping would also go on to make a sizable imprint on Hollywood and paved the way for other international films and nontraditional Hollywood movies like this to be made and viewed by a global audience. Yuen Woo-ping's sway even got his younger brother a job as an action choreographer on Daredevil (2003) with Ben Affleck.

The film's reach spread outside of cinema and into the gaming world, following its own diversification into that arena with a series of Matrix games. Notably, both Max Payne and indie first-person shooter Superhot incorporated Matrix-style effects. And this is all before you get to (inter)national lampoonery. Rob Schneider vehicle Deuce Bigalow: Male Gigolo (1999) was quick off the mark with its spoof of Trinity's suspended-animation crane kick. Scary Movie (2000), with another floating flo-mo crane kick pastiche, and Shrek (2001), showcasing Princess Fiona engaging in yet more bullet-time shenanigans, followed. Black Mirror creator Charlie Brooker even incorporated a reference mocking a news reporter "ignoring all the pricks milling around him like he's gliding through the fucking Matrix" later still in a 2010 episode of his satirical BBC *Newswipe* series.

You haven't made it until you've been sent up, and if the true badge of success is a string of parodies, then *The Matrix* can wear that pin with pride. All helped to lodge the movie in the global consciousness. Someone even re-created the famous lobby scene using peanuts in place of the actors. Bravo.

WILL SMITH DEEP FAKE

Making use of the latest in technology—in true
Matrix style—in 2019, YouTuber Shamook showed
us all what *The Matrix* would have looked like
had Will Smith accepted the Neo role in place of
Keanu Reeves. It showed Smith's Neo accepting
Morpheus's offer of the Red Pill, meeting with
Spoon Boy, halting a hail of bullets, and saving
Morpheus from the clutches of Agent Smith. Pretty
freaky, and confirmation that Smith made the right
decision, if anything. But then, another YouTube
user, Ctrl Shift Face, went one step further and
made an alternative deep fake resurrecting Bruce
Lee in the role. His video transferred Lee into the
fight training program to spar against Morpheus.
In this scene in the film, we see Neo pay homage
to Lee when he adopts Lee's signature nose touch
prior to continuing the fight.

Leaving a Legacy

Apart from setting a new bar for sci-fi actioners and bringing
martial arts movies like *Crouching Tiger, Hidden Dragon*, *Hero*,
House of Flying Daggers, and more not only to mainstream
audiences but also into Oscars territory, *The Matrix* introduced

a fair number of phrases into the lexicon, which is the sign of a truly influential work. Everyone knows what "A glitch in the Matrix," "There is no spoon," "Coppertop," "Red Pill," and "Blue Pill" mean, right? Not to mention the religion the film inspired.

MATRIXISM

A religion inspired by *The Matrix*, Matrixism, also known as the Path of the One, sprang up in 2004. Followers abided by the Four Tenets of Matrixism: belief in a messianic prophecy, use of psychedelic drugs, belief in a multilayered, semi-subjective reality, and adherence to the principles of at least one major religion. They used the Japanese kanji symbol for *red* as an emblem—a reference to both the Red Pill and the Matrix's green code, which was in part made up of Japanese symbols.

Still celebrated today, 2020 saw a limited collectors' edition, vinyl picture disc of the Don Davis–scored original soundtrack released, complete with jazzy Matrix code imagery on one side and Keanu Reeves in classic dual-gun Neo pose on the other. Over the years, the film has also been showered in accolades, ranking high on many esteemed publications' and critics' GOAT lists and even, as we've pointed out, securing its place in the National Film Registry.

Integrating personal insight, complex symbolic characterization, and big concepts with outstanding cutting-edge VFX and thrillingly precise balletic fight choreography, the Wachowskis' multilayered film is shot through with superiority. Never taking shortcuts or dropping the ball, and presenting everything in a way that speaks to all of us, the sibling luminaries created a work that was both of its time in a way few if any of its contemporaries managed and also ahead of its time. When we look back, despite *The Matrix*'s warnings, it can seem as though, as a species, we've sleepwalked to a point where tech is on the brink of taking over, and we're a step away from becoming the architects of our own impending demise. The sisters' opus still chimes loudly. Wake up, world. The Wachowskis are true visionaries, and this is, ultimately, why we love *The Matrix*.

THE WISDOM OF MORPHEUS

"I stand here before you now truthfully unafraid. Why? Because I believe something you do not? No, I stand here without fear because I remember. I remember that I am not here because of the path that lies before me but because of the path that lies behind me."